52
SUNDAYS

Other Books by Anthony Gooley

Bite Size Vatican II: A Very Basic Guide to the Council and its Four Constitutions.
St Paul's Publications: Strathfield.
2014.
ISBN 9781921963384

Deacons Today: New Wine & New Wineskins.
Coventry Press: Bayswater.
2019.
ISBN 9780648566151

The simplicity of this book is deceptive. Each week, we are guided into the fascinating story of the Mass which not only informs, but also turns the Mass into a prayer.

Bishop Greg Homeming, OCD
Bishop of Lismore

It is not uncommon to find Catholics in our pews who have been attending Mass for decades but remain unaware of the significance of what is taking place in the liturgy. In *Fifty-two Sundays, A Reflective Journey Through the Mass*, Dr Anthony Gooley provides his readers with a clear, accessible and well-illustrated introduction to the Mass that can bring the experience of the liturgy to life. It is theologically rich, whilst remaining easy to understand and will encourage the reader to engage in a full, conscious, and active participation in the Mass.

Deacon Peter Pellicaan PhD
Executive Director, Evangelisation Brisbane

Professor Gooley's reflective journey through the Mass accurately and lovingly offers an approachable and easy to absorb explanation of not only what happens in the Mass, but why it happens. The formative and transformative elements of the liturgy are presented in a way that conveys the missionary and evangelising nature of the Church – an assembly of baptised people 'called out' to bring Christ to all nations.

Dr Marco Ceccarelli
Director of the Centre for Faith Enrichment, Perth
Adjunct Senior Lecturer in Church History,
University of Notre Dame

52 SUNDAYS

A Reflective Journey through the Mass

ANTHONY GOOLEY

Published in Australia by
Coventry Press
33 Scoresby Road
Bayswater VIC 3153

ISBN 9781922589460

Copyright © Anthony Gooley 2024

All rights reserved. Other than for the purposes and subject to the conditions prescribed under the *Copyright Act*, no part of this publication may be reproduced, stored in a retrieval system, or transmitted in any form or by any means, electronic, mechanical, photocopying, recording or otherwise, without the prior permission of the publisher.

Nihil Obstat:	Reverend Gerard Diamond MA (Oxon), LSS, D.Theol.
	Diocesan Censor
Imprimatur:	Very Reverend Joseph Caddy AM Lic.Soc.Sci VG
	Vicar General
	Archdiocese of Melbourne
Date:	31 October 2023

The Nihil Obstat and Imprimatur are official declarations that a book or pamphlet is free of doctrinal or moral error. No implication is contained therein that those who have granted the Nihil Obstat and Imprimatur agree with the contents, opinions or statements expressed. They do not necessarily signify that the work is approved as a basic text for catechetical instruction.

Scripture quotations are from the Catholic edition of the *New Revised Standard Version Bible*, copyright 1965, 1966, Division of Christian Education of the National Council of the Churches of Christ in the United States of America. Used by permission. All rights reserved.

Catalogue-in-Publication entry is available from the National Library of Australia: http://catalogue.nla.gov.au

Cover design by Ian James – www.jgd.com.au
Text design by Coventry Press
Set in Tex Gyre Pagella
Printed in Australia

*For my wife,
my love and my faithful companion on the journey*

Contents

Introduction 9
1. Mass is a prayer 17
2. Where are you going? 21
3. Being Church 26
4. Preparation 30
5. Everybody has a part 34
6. Books, vessels and other stuff 38
7. Entering and centring 43
8. Procession 47
9. Singing 51
10. Silence 56
11. Bells and smells 60
12. Vestments 65
13. Praying with our body 69
14. Getting started 73
15. The Father is running to us 77
16. Lord, have mercy 81
17. Forgiveness and community 85
18. Thought, word and deed 89
19. Glory to God 93
20. Easter, every Sunday 97
21. Moving parts – opening prayer 101
22. Times and seasons 105
23. Two tables 112
24. Pairing the Word 116
25. A cycle within a cycle 121

26.	Welcoming the Gospel	126
27.	Receiving the Word	131
28.	I set my heart on...	135
29.	Calling to mind the Church and world	139
30.	Presenting ourselves	144
31.	Preparation of the Gifts	148
32.	Lift up your hearts	152
33.	Communion and being	156
34.	A mysterious exchange	163
35.	Preface	167
36.	Sanctus (Holy, Holy)	172
37.	It is right and just	175
38.	Great thanksgiving – Eucharistic Prayers	180
39.	Send down your Holy Spirit	184
40.	The Words of Institution	187
41.	The Mystery of Faith	192
42.	Great praise, Great Amen	195
43.	Sharing peace	199
44.	Praying as Jesus taught us	205
45.	Behold the Lamb of God	210
46.	A believer's prayer	215
47.	Corpus Christi procession	219
48.	What is it that you say Amen to?	224
49.	Cleaning the sacred vessels	229
50.	Reserving the Blessed Sacrament	232
51.	Moving parts – prayer after communion	236
52.	Sent on mission	240
A final word		245
Words to know		247
Further reading		260

Introduction

This book is not just dedicated to my wife, it is written for her. A little while back, my wife asked me if I would write a book about the Mass for ordinary folk to develop some sense of what we do and why. She mostly wanted it for her own reading but she believed that there would be lots of other people who would also benefit from such a book. Her thinking was that people might be more engaged and able to pray the Mass more effectively if they had a better understanding.

I am a theologian and my primary field is ecclesiology – the theology of the nature of the Church and its mission. I have written about Vatican II, about ministry, about Holy Orders and about the diaconate but I have not written much about worship. I am not a liturgist, a scholar who specialises in the study of worship. So, I decided that any book I would write for her and for you about the Mass would not be the kind of book an expert liturgist would write.

Fifty-two Sundays is my meditation on the Mass as it is celebrated in the Ordinary form of the Latin or Roman Rite. There may be some technical things about the Mass that you might learn from this book but my intention is not to explore the technicalities of Mass. I start my reflections where the Mass begins and I finish my reflections when the Mass ends and I comment on some of the parts in between. I primarily wanted to get behind what we say and do to expose the theology and spirituality that is behind it all. I wanted this to be a book that would help you pray the Mass and be prayerful at Mass and to shape your way of living the Christian life because you have encountered the Mass. I hope my reflections will be a stimulus to your own personal reflections and contribute to deepening your own appreciation of and participation in Mass.

More than anything, this book is meant as an aid to forming what might be called a liturgical spirituality. This is a spirituality that is grounded in the experience of worship and which continues that experience into the lived reality of your own world and its context. Liturgy, the public worship of the Church, is profoundly connected to the public living of the Gospel in my view. Liturgy, of which the Mass is a supreme example, connects us with one another and with God through a living encounter with Jesus in the Holy Spirit. Liturgy deepens our communion with God and with one another and compels us toward mission. Communion and mission are two sides of the same Catholic coin.

This book is for my wife, as I mentioned already, but as I began to think about how I might approach the task, I had in mind a wider audience. I had in mind everyday Catholics who go to Mass, including the bishops, presbyters and deacons. The Mass is the prayer of Christ, with, through and in his Body the Church. So all of us who participate are those who need to nurture a liturgical spirituality and who need to meditate on what we say and do in the Mass. A bishop, no less than the

Introduction

person in the pew, is someone who can profit spiritually from reflecting on what we do and say at Mass. We can all pray the Mass better by praying with our heart and mind in harmony with our voice and our body. As important as technicalities and rules are for the Mass, without a spiritual dimension the words and gestures can become outward shows. This book is for all Catholics who go to Mass – clergy and laity alike – because we all have that same need to connect these dimensions.

I think the book would be helpful for those who are learning about the Catholic faith or are on a journey into the Catholic Church. Perhaps there are Christians who are making the journey into full communion with the Catholic Church or people who are not baptised and are entering through the Rite of Christian Initiation of Adults, who may find this book helps them learn to engage with the Catholic Mass.

What the experience of the celebration of Mass is like at any given parish can be quite varied. Some parishes have a liturgy team that prepare the liturgy. There may be great attention to detail and the flow of the liturgy in such parishes. Some have a wonderful choir and music director and they produce beautiful and engaging music for the congregation to sing. Some will have properly trained and installed lay ministries of lector and acolyte or perhaps readers and senior servers. Some will use incense at all the indicated places and make use of other symbols in a rich and bold way that engages all of the senses in the act of worship.

In some Masses, there will be preaching that can set hearts on fire and inspire and lift up the congregation. There may be a presider whose words and gestures are in such harmony with his spirit that the prayerfulness of the congregation is fostered. There will be some congregations who can lift the roof off the Church with the full-throated singing of the parts of the Mass and hymns. There can be parish Masses where it seems so obvious that the whole of Christ's body – the laity, deacon, presbyter and bishop – seem to pray together with one heart.

There can be all of these experiences I have suggested above. All of them are possible. For many this is not the experience of Mass. Instead, there are few resources to support good liturgy. Music is supplied by some faithful volunteers doing the best they can with the resources they have, including a limited vocal and musical range. Prayers are said hastily and without much preparation or attention to how they may best be prayed. Someone is asked at the last minute to read and perhaps has seen the text for the first time when they arrive before Mass begins. There may be a preacher who has not prepared and rambles on in some off the top of his head monologue, hoping no one will notice or that something good may come of his words by accident. The symbols and symbolism may be mean and small. Music may be unsingable or, when it is singable, no one sings. And as for incense, that is too often reserved for funerals. It may appear as if we are all just a bunch of individuals who happen to be at Mass.

Introduction

I can't control whether your experience of Mass is going to be the best of kinds or the worst of kinds, the grandest of kinds or the simplest of kinds, but I can assure you that no matter how badly or how beautifully it is celebrated, the grace of the Mass is there to be received by those who are disposed and open to God's grace. We can have some control over our disposition for Mass and be attentive in mind and heart to the riches of the texts and the gestures; and allow these to shape us into the Body of Christ that we receive at Mass.

The Mass has its own dynamic that equips us to live the Christian life. The Mass calls us together into the communion of Christ's body as the assembly gathers. The Word of God we hear in the Scriptures proclaimed, forms us as disciples. The Eucharist continues our transformation into what we have received – the body of Christ. The Mass sends us on mission. Always the same dynamic: called, formed, transformed and sent. No matter how splendidly (and I wish it was always as splendid as our resources could make it) or how simple, Mass is always a participation in this dynamic. It will always be this way because it is a participation in the Body of Christ in his mission and in his dying and rising.

How to read this book. I have called the book *Fifty-two Sundays* because that is the way I suggest you read it. It is not meant to be read from cover to cover in one sitting. There are fifty-two sections which begin at the start of the Mass and work through the Mass more or less in the order that we encounter things. I write a reflection about each of these parts. Some of the reflections are only about five hundred words long and some just a bit over a thousand. My idea is that you will read one section and then experience it at Mass and commence your own reflection on that part. You may find that your reflections take you in very different directions from mine and what I have had to say may serve merely as a springboard for your own pondering.

The years 2020-2021 were strange years in which to complete this book. A global pandemic kept so many of us away from participation in Mass. As the world recovers and Mass with a full congregation becomes possible again, I hope this little book will contribute in its own way to recovery in what will certainly be a new normal. Perhaps the Mass you have missed out on for so long can become a deeper experience now that we are able to participate in person once again.

Finally, this book is a journey. I went on a journey as I slowly wrote this book over a long period of time. I reflected on my experience of Mass and I reflected on the key documents about the Mass. I pondered and I prayed and when I had pondered a little more, I would write some. I wrote it in the order of the Mass because my reflections followed that same way. I would like to invite you to walk some of this journey with me. I did not go back and rewrite sections in the light of what I wrote later because I wanted the reflections to remain fresh. The sections are not necessarily connected except that they are parts of the Mass. My hope is that you will write your own reflections following mine; if not literally, at least as you ponder the Mass, write it in your heart.

Third Sunday in Advent, 2023

A note about the Bible

Throughout this book, I use First Testament and Second Testament to refer to what we commonly call the Old and New Testaments. I do so for a number of reasons. First, 'new' can sometimes be understood to mean replacing something that is 'old'. It does not. Secondly, because some use the terms Hebrew Scriptures for the First Testament and Christian Scriptures for the Second Testament and these terms are misleading. First, misleading because Catholic and Orthodox Christians use the Greek version of the Bible, the Septuagint, and it has more books in the First Testament than the Hebrew version. The Septuagint is the version used by those who wrote the Second Testament. We know this because they quote the Greek rather than Hebrew versions of most texts. Secondly, misleading because both the First and Second Testaments are Christian Scriptures. One of our first heresies that was condemned said that only the Second Testament is Christian Scripture.

1

Mass is a prayer

When I was a young boy but old enough to head off to Mass by myself, without my parents, my mother had a way of checking out if I had actually managed to get myself there and had not in fact pretended to go. She would ask, upon my return home, 'Who said Mass today?' By this she meant which priest had presided at Mass. We had a number of priests[1] (presbyters) in our Cathedral parish and any of them could have been the presider. Which priest was to preside on Sunday was printed in the parish bulletin. Of course, if I did not have access to the parish bulletin, I could not know for certain, and by this she hoped to confirm my presence or otherwise at Mass.

I have learned a lot about Mass since then and have attended many of them on Sundays, weekdays,

---

1 Both a bishop and a presbyter have priestly functions. Catholics are in the habit of calling presbyters (which means elder in Koine Greek) priests but I will use the term Vatican II tried to recover to make the distinctions clearer.

weddings, funerals and feast days. If she were to ask me that same question, 'Who said Mass today?', I would be far better equipped to respond. The answer is impressive and inspiring. Knowing it will change the way we celebrate Mass and assist us to receive the grace that flows from participation in it.

The Catholic Mass or Celebration of the Eucharist, as it is also known, is a prayer. It is also called a liturgy, which is a Greek word for the public worship of the Church. The answer to the question, who said Mass today is Christ Jesus. More specifically, Mass is the prayer of Christ praying in, with and through his Body the Church. The presbyter or bishop who presides and the people assembled continue the work of Christ in the Mass. Through their words, gestures, silence and presence. Christ is praying in his Body the Church, through the Holy Spirit, to the Father.

As a prayer, Mass is different to our private prayer. The most important difference is that it is necessarily public prayer and common prayer. We celebrate Mass together in a public forum. The whole Church – head (presider) and body (deacon and congregation) – 'says Mass' together, celebrates Mass together and prays together, as if in one voice. This is corporate worship. We do not gather as individuals participating in the same thing, like an audience at a movie or concert. When we gather at Mass, we gather as what we are, the Body of Christ. Whereas private prayer may be something we do alone in our room, chapel, at the beach or some other place, liturgical prayer always means 'we and Jesus time' not 'me and Jesus time'. In reality, even the private prayer of a Christian is not 'alone' time because they are always a part of the Body of Christ, and never lose that connection.

Prayer, both public and private, has five dimensions that are worth keeping in mind. (You can remember five because most people have five fingers. The four P's on your fingers and the A on your thumb, may help you remember.) These five dimensions are presence, place, praise, petition and adoration. We will look at these five in relation to public prayer or liturgy.

In public prayer, we need to be mindful first that we are in God's Holy *Presence* and secondly to be mindful of the *presence* of our brothers and sisters in Christ. Mass is very much together time, not alone time for private devotions. We celebrate our Mass (normally) in a designated sacred *place*, a Church. When we celebrate Mass, we should take time to notice the place that we are in as well as those who are present to us. It is good to get some sense, before we pray the Mass, that we are in a sacred space. Prayer takes on three general forms, although these forms can be expressed in many different ways. Liturgical prayer will always have some aspect of *praise*. We gather to offer praise and worship to God. We are acting out what the commandments say – to worship God alone and worship no one or nothing else. Linked closely to praise is also the attitudes and words of thanksgiving. We will see later just how central thanksgiving is to the Mass. In the public prayer of the Mass, we always offer *petitions* for the needs of the Church and the world and we can also come with and pray for our own particular petitions. During some of the silent times of the Mass – especially after communion – we can pray our own petitions to God in the silence of our hearts. Finally, *adoration* always has a part to play in the public prayer of the Church. We come to adore God's Holy Presence. Adoration carries with it a sense of being in awe, and of turning our gaze outward and not focusing on our inner world but the Holy Presence of God around us.

If we become more conscious of Mass as the preeminent expression of the public prayer of the Church in which we participate, we come to Mass with a different awareness than what we bring to private prayer. We are more consciously aware of the other, of those who have been baptised into Christ and who, together with me, are part of the Body of Christ. It is not only this 'horizontal' awareness of my sisters and brothers – for want of a better expression – but also the 'vertical' awareness that it is God who has called us to this assembly and we have gathered in his Holy Presence, in a most startling and direct way. When we go to Mass to pray as the Body of Christ, it is as if we are standing right there in the Holy of Holies, where God's Presence in experienced as a living reality of grace. Perhaps before going to Mass next time, you could spend a little time in private prayer, pondering what we have reflected on here to prepare yourself to enter into this public work of the Church.

2

Where are you going?

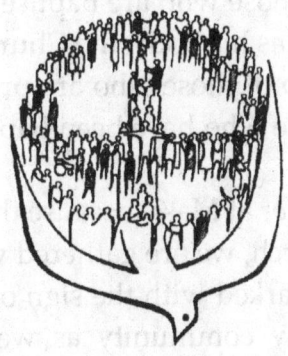

When my son was at university as an undergraduate, getting him (or his sister) to Mass was always a difficult proposition. One Sunday morning as I was heading out the door, I heard him call out, 'Where are you going?' I could have given him a direct and simple answer that I was going to Mass but instead I replied, 'I am going to Mt Zion, the city of the Living God, the heavenly Jerusalem' (Hebrews 12:22).[2] He probably did not even hear what I said or, if he did, he would not have made sense of it.

---

2 Unless indicated otherwise the Scripture quotes come from the Revised Standard Version.

The Letter to the Hebrew, in the Second Testament,[3] is a profound meditation on Christ the High Priest and the nature of Christian worship. In the previous section we reflected on the public nature of the Mass as the Prayer of the Church. We noted that when we gather, we do so with Christ and with those who are baptised and constituted in the Holy Spirit as his Body, the Church. The Church is not only made up of those who are present in the Mass today but all those who have been baptised and all who will be baptised.

When we gather at Mass, because this is the prayer of Christ in his Church, we are gathered with all who have gone before us marked with the sign of faith. We gather with the heavenly community as well as the earthly Church community. All of the angels and saints and martyrs in heaven and Mary the Mother of God and her beloved spouse Joseph, are just as present to us as the women, men, and children gathered in the parish Church.

When we enter a Catholic Church, we will see images of the Mother of God (*Theotokos*), saints and martyrs and perhaps angels too. There may be statues, paintings, stained glass windows or icons which capture their images. The primary purpose of these images is to remind us that when we gather at Mass on Sunday, they gather with us too. When we participate in the Eucharist,

---

3 The Bible has two main divisions, the Old Testament and the New Testament. I refer to them as the First and the Second Testament because 'Old' can sound like its outdated or superseded and that is not what the word 'New' is meant to convey.

they participate with us. The saints are as much a part of the gathered community and participants in the Mass as we who are gathered in the Church.

There are many more saints in the Church than those who have been canonised or officially recognised. Some of them may attend Mass with you now and their sanctity may be glimpsed by you and truly known to God. They may never become one of the canonised saints. Along with these unnamed saints are all the un-named women and men who have been baptised and died. They too remain part of the Body of Christ, the Church. Therefore, they too are among those who are gathered for the Feast of the Lamb, which is the Eucharist or Mass.

How extraordinary it is to think that when we gather for Mass, we are gathering with the community of heaven too. Not only that, but, if we follow the logic of the Letter to the Hebrews, we are standing in the Holy of Holies, the place in the First Testament language that meant the Divine Presence of God. In the Jewish world of Jesus' earthly ministry, the Jews offered sacrifice in the Temple in Jerusalem. The Temple was divided into a number of areas, the most holy of which was called the Holy of Holies (Most Holy Place). This place represented the Divine Presence and once each year the High Priest could enter here to offer sacrifice for the forgiveness of the sins of Israel. He walked into this place through a great curtain, sometimes called the veil of the temple.

Hebrews tells us that when we come to celebrate the Mass, we all walk through the curtain into the Holy of Holies and stand in the Divine Presence. The way has been opened for us via a new curtain, which is the flesh of Christ. In chapter 10:19-22 of that letter, we read, 'Therefore, brothers and sisters, since we have confidence to enter the Most Holy Place by the blood of Jesus, by a new and living way opened for us through the curtain, that is, his body, and since we have a great priest over the house of God, let us draw near to God with a sincere heart and with the full assurance that faith brings...'

At Mass, we are going to stand in the Heavenly Jerusalem and then keep walking up the Holy Mountain into the Temple and then through the curtain into the Most Holy Place. We can do so because we have been baptised and it is Christ that we have put on (Romans 12:5) and together we are parts of one another. We are not just going to Mass. We are making a profound spiritual pilgrimage and we start that pilgrimage in our local Church. No matter how humble or how grand that building may be, it is the place of pilgrimage where we start the ascent to the Holy City, the Heavenly Jerusalem.

When you next go to Mass, take a moment to take in the privilege that you have been called to enter into this Holy Place. Examine the art works and images carefully and slowly to help you develop a sense of the wider group of others who gather with you. Perhaps bring to mind some of those you know who were baptised and have died. Recall their presence with you. Take some time to ponder in awe the great mystery that you have been called – along with all who are gathered here – to stand in God's Presence and minister to him. You are standing with all these others in the Most Holy Place. In the First

Testament, only the High Priest could enter this place once each year and even then, he could not lift his gaze. He remained bowed and with eyes averted. Yet each time we enter Mass, we can stand in the exact place in the sacramental mystery of the celebration. Ponder what you have come to and where you are going. With the psalmist, pray 'I rejoiced when I heard them say, let us go to God's house' (Psalm 122:1).

3
Being Church

Sometimes Christians may be heard to say that they are going to church on Sunday. For Latin Catholics, that's a way of saying 'I am going to Mass'. Eastern Catholics and Orthodox Christians may mean the Divine Liturgy, which is their name for the Mass. Going to church is being used as a kind of synonym for attending public worship in other words. It is a little misleading, though, to use such language, because we are not going to church but being Church when we gather for Mass.

I am not sure when in our history Christians started to call the places in which we gather for worship a church. It is certainly not how the word church was being used in the first four centuries of the Christian era. It must have developed sometime after that. Christians did not originally have a name for the place in which they gathered for worship. Before Christianity became a legal option in the ancient Roman empire, Christians gathered in large homes of members or in caves, where they could safely worship. Once Christianity was tolerated and eventually made the religion of the Empire, usually they would gather in what we might call a town hall today, a basilica. Sometime later, former pagan temples were converted to use for Christian worship. Even then, the places were not called churches.

The English word church comes via the Koine Greek *ecclesia* (ek-lair-see-a), which means those who are called to assemble or the assembly. The key point is that the word Church originally meant the people who are baptised and did not mean a place at all.

The Koine Greek word ecclesia is a compound word *ek* and *leuo* (lay-o) which means to be called out from. Christ has called a people out from among all the nations to be a people of his own. He does not just call us as individuals but as a community, 'a chosen people, a royal priesthood, a holy nation, God's special possession' (1 Peter 2:9). From the beginning of creation God had intended the Church to be. It was prepared for in the assembly of Israel, the Jews who are our foremothers and forefathers in faith. In his own earthly ministry, Christ actively laid the foundations for the manifestation of the Church and the Holy Spirit gave life to and continues to give life to the Church.

In the Second Testament, the Church is revealed as the Body of Christ (in Latin that is *Corpus Christi*). All who are baptised are baptised into the Body of Christ and become part of one another (1 Corinthians 12:27, Romans 12:5, Ephesians 5:23). That is, baptism is both a communion with Christ and a communion with those who are also baptised into him. Our Eucharist is a participation in the Body of Christ too. When we are baptised, we become the Body of Christ. When we assemble for the Mass, we are not so much going to church as being the Church.

The Second Vatican Council (1962-65) taught that the Church (i.e., we who are baptised) are in Christ like a sacrament (*Lumen Gentium* n. 1). We are a sacrament of intimate communion between humanity and God; and the communion and unity of the whole human race. We, the Church, are both a sign of this communion and the means by which such communion comes into effect. When we gather for Mass, we are in effect being that sacrament of communion and being what we are called to be by God.

As we assemble at Mass, it is worth taking some time to ponder all of the women, men and children gathered with us. Some are young and some are old. Some are in the full vigour of health and others perhaps sick, or just frail or stooped with aged. Some may be ethnically related to Irish, English, Italian, Maltese, Croatian, Russian, Greek, Tongan, Chinese, Indian, Vietnamese, Nigerian, an Aboriginal or Torres Strait Islander or many other cultures, languages and groups. Some may be rich and some poor. Some may be well educated and others, perhaps, with minimal education. They possibly cover a wide range of political views and allegiances too. They are a very diverse group who may gather with us at Mass on Sunday, at least in most Australian parishes. Globally the Catholic Church is the most culturally diverse religious group on the planet. It has been said that most of the world's major language groups are represented within the communion of the Catholic Church.

As you look at this diverse group, ponder the fact that each one of them is a part of you because you are each part of the Body of Christ. These are your sisters and brothers. In the Mass, you will touch the Body of Christ before you have received the Eucharist (Holy Communion). You will touch the Body of Christ at the exchange of peace before Holy Communion. Like you, these others are being the Church, when they assemble for Mass. Perhaps at no other time in the week is this reality made clearer to you than at Mass. The assembly reminds you that you have been called by Christ and that you have responded to that call and you continue to remain in his Body the Church along with all who are present. At Mass, you get some taste of what it is to be Church. To savour this taste more fully, you need not only to look at the others as those who are part of me, you need to love these others. Deep, positive regard for each person present will help each of us be more clearly Church. The world will be drawn closer to us (the Church) if they see how much we love one another. If you cannot love the sister and brother that you can see, what hope is there for a deeper love of God whom you cannot see? (1 John 4:20-21) Being Church makes greater demands of us than going to church.

4
Preparation

When we are going out with family and friends to celebrate a special birthday, a graduation from university, a special wedding anniversary and many similar events, there is a lot of preparation that goes into the event before we arrive. Even if we are simply going to be a guest at the event, we begin to prepare ourselves sometimes well before we arrive. We may be thinking about the appropriate clothes to wear or a gift we wish to present and how we will present it. On the day itself, we plan our timing so that we are all dressed and ready to attend with plenty of time. The preparation for the event becomes part of the total experience of the occasion.

Mass is the most important occasion in the week of a Catholic. Since it is such an important occasion it deserves some effort to prepare well. You don't just want to stumble into it and arrive unprepared. You would not do that for a fiftieth wedding anniversary celebration so why would you do this for Mass? As with all these things, prepare as best as you can but accept also the reality of the limitations of your personal and family situation. The last thing that you want to do is to stress out about being prepared.

In the week leading up to Mass, perhaps we can begin preparing by reading the Scripture portions that are to read at Mass. Many parishes provide the reference in the parish bulletin the week before. You can also purchase a Mass book or missal with all of the readings. A missal also has the prayers of the Mass.

Perhaps you or your family could read the Gospel on Monday night when you have your evening meal. On Tuesday, the first reading and, on Wednesday, the second reading. As we shall see later, the readings for Mass are chosen in that order. On each of these nights, you could conclude the reading by reading one of the prayers of the Mass.

If you want to prepare more deeply, you could read one of the commentaries on either the lectionary (the readings for the week) or perhaps just a commentary on the Gospel. There are many Gospel commentaries around and some of these are written for people with no specialist knowledge of the Bible. Commentaries help readers understand the meaning of the passage and provide some explanation of technical terms and the context of the passage.

When you read the Scripture portions and prayers, savour the words. Take note of the themes and common ideas that grab your attention. What are they saying to you? What are they saying to the Church? Do they speak to the issues and situations emerging in our society and culture?

On the day you attend Mass, prepare yourself before you leave home. Take a moment to ponder how awesome it is that you have been called to celebrate the Mass, that Christ will pray through, with and in you, in the unity of the Holy Spirit to the glory of God the Father. Take a moment to ponder that you have been called and you have accepted to participate in the work of Christ for the salvation of all the world. That quiet moment of reflection may be as you are having a morning coffee or breakfast or as you shower and get dressed for Mass. Just some moments of recollection are all that is required.

Think also about how you and your family will dress. Things like climate, the weather today, culture and many other things may shape some of your decisions about how you dress. In some cultures, it is still an expectation that we put on 'our Sunday best' to go to Mass. In other places, smart, casual attire is acceptable. The main point is that you think about where you are going and how you wish to present yourself. Be a little thoughtful. Balance that with the reality of trying to get little children ready for Mass and whether or not a tense moment about a child's clothing choice is worth the stress and balance that against the fact that they are at least coming to Mass with you.

When thinking about how you dress or how others present themselves at Mass, keep in mind that God does not judge by appearance but what is in the heart. A dirty, smelly person with unwashed clothes and the person with impeccable fashion sense and expensive clothes are both judged the same in God's eyes. The thinking about how you dress is merely about mindfulness about where I am going and what I am doing. It is part of preparation and cultivation of a proper disposition for Mass not a fashion statement.

Upon arriving at Mass, spend a moment in prayer asking God for the grace of a proper disposition for celebrating today. Pray that you will be attentive to the words, the gestures, the music and singing. Pray that you will be attentive to the awesome mystery in which you are to participate. Pray that you will be mindful of your sisters and brothers in Christ, with whom you gather. Pray that your participation in the Mass will bear fruit in your life, evidenced by a life transformed by the grace of Mass.

Preparation for Mass is about preparing the heart, mind and body. Preparing the heart is about trying to create a proper disposition that will allow us to enter fully into the celebration and then go on mission at the end. Preparing the mind can happen through attentiveness to the Scripture portions and the prayers and pondering their meaning. Preparation of the body includes how we dress, how we enter and how we actively take part in the celebration, mindful that because we are baptised, we are part of the Body of Christ, the Church.

5
Everybody has a part

There is a very big difference between attending a sporting event, concert or sitting in a movie theatre and being with a group of people at Mass. The group of people who attend a sports event are not out on the field as players. Those at a concert or movie are all spectators. Everyone who attends Mass is a participant. Mass is definitely not a spectator sport. Unlike a concert, every person at Mass is part of the 'orchestra', the 'band', or the 'cast'. Everybody has a part to play at Mass.

All of those who are fully initiated Catholics, that is, they have been baptised, confirmed/chrismated, and received first Holy Communion participate as one priestly people in the sacrifice of the Mass. The presider is not 'saying' Mass while the deacons, acolyte, readers, ushers, choir and congregation sit and listen. The presbyter or bishop who presides is doing just that, presiding. Everyone – the presider, deacon, acolyte, choir, ushers and all the congregation – are saying and praying the Mass together, with one voice.

The Second Vatican Council called for full, conscious and active participation of the whole church, clergy and laity, in the celebration of the Mass. This does not mean that only those with a defined role – presider, deacon, acolyte, sever etc. – are being active and the rest are not. The whole of the Church is actively participating, each according to her or his assigned part.

If we return to the orchestra example and invert it with regard to the Mass, then we have a very useful way of understanding full, conscious and active participation. All the people at Mass are like the orchestra. Each person contributes to the whole symphony their words, gestures, presence etc. not as discrete notes but as a blended harmony of sound. We have to imagine that we are the 'orchestra' and everyone is on stage and performing.

Full participation does not mean that everyone gets to play the trumpet or the drums – to continue our orchestra analogy. Each of us should fully play the role that we are assigned. The presider, deacon, acolyte, musician, choir and the whole congregation each has a different 'instrument' to play and contribute to the whole. We should not play another person's instrument or even desire to do so. If we don't play our own part, then we may end up with a very discordant sound and not a pleasant melody.

Conscious means to be aware and attentive to what it is that we are doing. It is easy for us to drift off with our attention focused on how someone is dressed, what

I need to buy at the shop to cook for lunch or some cute baby in the front row. That can happen to all of us, clergy and laity alike, but we need to call ourselves back to attention. An aspect of conscious and attentive is to try to resist doing things by rote and perhaps without feeling and energy. We need to savour the words as we pray them, become conscious of our gestures and what they mean and that we do them well. To sing with a full voice and attention to the lyrics. Perhaps we need to cultivate in our imagination an idea that we are doing and saying all these things as if it was the first time.

I remember hearing a very old, retired presbyter say to a newly ordained one, 'If you pray every Mass with the devotion and care of your first one, then all will go well. You will never forget the awesome privilege and you will grow in holiness'. That is good advice for the deacon and laity too. Praying with devotion and care as if it were the very first time you have encountered Mass.

Active does not mean everyone must have a special job to do. Every member is active from the moment she/he enters the Church. Attentive listening to the Word of God is active. Singing with a robust and full voice is active. Responding to the prayers and antiphons, kneeling, sitting and crossing yourself, processing up to receive communion and sitting in silence, are all aspects of being active.

Are you aware of your part? Do you think you are an active and conscious participant in Mass? Do you think 'Father is saying Mass and I am just in the congregation'? That little word, 'just', is a word that minimises what I truly am. I am a part of God's priestly people offering Mass for the peace and salvation of all the world. That is no small task on a Sunday. How many of your friends, neighbours and relatives are doing something this profound with some of their time on the weekend?

When you look about you at Mass, become aware that these women and men and children, including you, are the instruments Christ has chosen to be his voice, his gestures and his prayer to God the Father in the communion of the Holy Spirit. Everybody has a part to play at Mass. It is not a spectator sport. Each time you take your place in the Church or perhaps just as you are about to walk in, ask God for the grace for you to know how can you better play your part.

6

Books, vessels and other stuff

There are lots of things needed for the celebration of Mass such as cloths, books, candles and lots of other things which we may or may not notice and perhaps not know what they are and why we use them. Altar servers, clergy and those who act as sacristans (those who prepare everything for Mass) may be very familiar with them but many others not. In this section, we explore some of these.

Let's start with cloth. Most of us would be aware that there is a large table cloth, called the altar cloth, that covers the whole altar. They are cleaned and replaced regularly. We only leave the altar without this cloth from Holy Thursday night until we commence the eucharist at the Holy Saturday Paschal Vigil. Before the bread and wine is placed on the altar, another square white cloth, called a corporal, is placed on top of this and the chalice (cup) and the paten (plate) are placed on this cloth. It is called a corporal because the word for body in Latin is *corpus* and the function of this cloth is to catch any fragments of the Body and Blood of Christ. It is simply easier to remove one small cloth than to change the whole altar cloth if fragments fall or drops spill.

The server, acolyte or deacon will also provide the presider with a rectangular-shaped white cloth called a purifier. This sits beside the chalice. It is used to wipe any drops of wine and later will be used wipe down the pattern and chalice. This cloth is removed when the chalice and paten leave the altar. The other cloth that the server will give the presider is a finger towel, which he uses to wipe his fingers after washing them.

Sometimes you may see a stiff, white, linen board (*burse*) placed on top of the chalice. It is not essential for Mass. It simply has the practical function of keeping flies and bugs out of the chalice. If there are no flies you don't require the board. Over this you may sometimes see another optional cloth cover, which is in the liturgical colour of the day. It may be placed over the chalice and paten before and after Mass.

Several books are used for the Mass. The readings from Scripture are printed in a book called a lectionary (book of readings). This book only contains the portions of the Bible to be read at Mass and not the whole Bible. Sometimes the deacon will bring in and place on the altar, and later read from, a more elaborate looking book called the Book of Gospels (Evangeliary). This contains all of the Gospel portions to be read in Mass.

The large book that is placed on the altar when the gifts of bread and wine are brought up is the Roman Missal, sometimes called a sacramentary. It contains all of the fixed and moveable prayers and rituals for Mass that are required for the whole liturgical year. It has words printed in black and these are the words that are to be chanted or spoken by the presider, deacon and people. There are other words printed in red and these are the instructions about gestures and what to do at any particular time of the Mass. These red words are called rubrics, from the Latin word (*ruber*) for red.

Candles are a sign and reminder of many things: the resurrection of Christ who is the light of the world and of our own baptism. Normally, there are two on or near the altar. If a bishop presides in his Cathedral, there may be seven candles. This is not to honour the bishop. They represent the seven lamp stands referred to in the Book of Revelation and Christ who stands among them. The bishop stands as a sign of Christ, a living icon of his presence. Which is why a bishop commences Mass with the Easter greeting of Christ to the disciples: 'Peace be with you' and not 'the Lord be with you' as a presbyter would.

During the fifty days of Easter, the Paschal Candle, the sign of Christ rising from the dead, is placed near the Table of the Word. The Table of the Word (Ambo) is the place from which the Scriptures are proclaimed. The larger table is the Table of Eucharist (altar). This candle is consecrated at the Paschal Vigil each year and is decorated with signs that speak to us of salvation and resurrection and the continuing presence of Christ. During the rest of the year, it is placed near the baptism font. Baptism candles are always lit from the Paschal

Candle. We place the Paschal Candle by a coffin at funerals as a reminder of our sure and certain hope of resurrection.

Apart from the processional cross, there may be another cross or crucifix in the space near the altar (sanctuary). A crucifix is a cross with a body fixed to it or painted on it. These remind us that the Mass is a participation in and not a repetition of the one sacrifice of Christ. It is his death and resurrection and looking forward to his coming again that we celebrate in every Mass.

The water and wine for Mass are presented in small jugs. The water jug needs to only hold a tiny amount of water and may be very small. The size of the jug for the wine will depend on how much wine is needed. Some dioceses observe the custom of making bread and wine available for all at communion time and some only share the cup with a few people, perhaps just the presider, deacon, acolytes and extraordinary ministers of communion. It is actually a more complete sign if most people can receive both at communion time.

There are some items of furniture every Catholic church will have. A place from which the readings are proclaimed is called the Ambo. There will be an altar. There will be a large, and sometimes ornate chair for the one who is presiding to sit on. This is called the Presidents Chair. In a Cathedral, there will be a large ornate chair called the cathedra, which is the chair of the bishop. Cathedral takes its name from this chair and normally a diocese takes its name from where the city in which the chair is located. By tradition, a bishop may sit in this chair for preaching but, for practical reasons, rarely do so. No one but the diocesan bishop may sit in that chair because it is a symbol of his leadership over the local Church (diocese).

A deacon will be seated at the right hand of the bishop or priest. The deacon traditionally is the bishops 'right hand man' helping the bishop look over the local church (diocese) and keeping him informed about the needs of the Church and the other people who live in the boundaries of the local Church. Other clergy are arranged in the sanctuary in such a way as not to obscure the views of most of the congregation. Altar servers and acolytes will normally sit to the side and away from clergy so that it is clear who is who and to allow them most ease to perform their duties in the Mass.

When you enter your church or a new one, it is worth taking some time to orient yourself toward the basic layout of the place. Ponder why it is that we take such special care to provide clean and beautiful items to use. We want to have a worthy celebration and a beautiful celebration. Beauty, order and simplicity characterise the way Mass is celebrated in the Latin or Roman Rite.

7

Entering and centring

Lots of places and cultures have rites or ways of entering a place and marking a transition from the outside to the inside or from one activity to another. In some places, guests take off their shoes at the door of a house. Before entering a mosque (masjid), shoes are removed and there are washings to be performed. The main purpose of such rituals is to mark our transition from the ordinary life to prepare us to enter into the world of spiritual worship. The rituals help us become more mindful of what it is that we have come to do.

In a Latin Catholic Church, the main ritual for entry is tracing the sign of the cross on our bodies with holy water (Eastern Catholics may make the sign without the water). The sign of the cross is the very first ritual the community of the Church – the minister, your parents and god-parents – performed on you as you entered the

Church for the Rite of Baptism. Normally this first ritual is performed outside the entrance to the church. The rite of Baptism, as you know, involves immersion or pouring of water and the invocation of the Holy Trinity: Father, Son and Holy Spirit.

When you enter a Catholic Church, you combine these rituals with the tracing of the cross and the use of water (at least in pre-COVID times), to remind you of your baptism. The Sacrament of Baptism is the door of the Church and the door of faith (Latin *porta fidei*). It is the means by which you entered the Body of Christ, the Church. Each new entry into a church is a recollection of baptism and a recommitment to the life of faith in Christ. In some churches, this is brought out more deeply because the water container for the entry ritual is the baptism font.

Sometimes, it is worth pausing and making that entry sign of the cross a little more slowly. Take time to really notice what you are doing. Feel the water as you dip your fingers. Notice the points as your fingertips trace the sign on your body. Focus on each word... in the name... of the Father... and of the Son... and of the Holy Spirit. Even that first phrase, 'in the name' is filled with deep meaning. In the ancient world of our Jewish and Christian ancestors, the phase was another way of saying 'in the [Divine] Presence'. It is a reminder that we have come to be in the Divine Presence. We have since ancient times named this Presence as Father, Son and Holy Spirit. You have come here today to be in the Holy Presence of God, to touch the Presence in a mysterious way through the celebration of

Mass. Later you will receive into your hand and on your lips the Real Presence of Christ.

The second entry ritual is a genuflection – or bow, if you are unable to genuflect. Focus on the altar as you make this ritual. Very early in the Christian era, probably within a few years after the death and resurrection of Jesus, our ancestors in faith took text from Scripture, Isaiah 23 that had been written about God the Father and applied it to Jesus (Philippians 2:4-11), that he would have the name above every name and that at his name all would bend the knee or bow down. That is what we are doing in our genuflection or bow. The text says that all will call him [Jesus] Lord. Here they are applying the Divine Name to Jesus. As they did 2000 years ago, so you do now.

Now that you have entered, it is time to become centred. Take some time (if your children permit) to sit quietly and to take a moment to recite a prayer as a repeated phrase. It could be as simple as 'I am in the Holy Presence of God' or 'Here I am, Lord, I come to do your will'. Use this time to transition from home, the car park and a busy morning to become still and centred on God.

You are not alone here. You are part of the Body of Christ. All those who have been baptised into Christ are part of one another. Take a moment to notice some men, some women, some children and as you look at each recite, 'The Body of Christ, my brother. The body of Christ, my sister.' Begin to notice those who are a part of you. Pray that you will come to love them deeply and join your prayer with them to God in this holy liturgy.

Pray that you and they will become what we truly are, the Body of Christ.

If you can focus each week a little more on how you enter and how you centre in Mass, then perhaps each week you will be more greatly disposed to recognising Christ truly present, in the assembly, in the ordained ministers, in the Scripture proclaimed and, most importantly, as he is truly present in the Eucharist which you will receive. Be present in order to be in the Divine Presence.

8
Procession

Mass begins with an entrance procession. The purpose of the procession is not to elevate the presider and make him the focus of attention. The real purpose is twofold. First, we want to be gathered together in mind and heart around the purpose for which we have assembled, the praise of God and offering the sacrifice of the Mass. Second, the procession reminds us that we are a pilgrim people, we are companions on the journey toward the Kingdom of God. Several elements help us comprehend this twofold purpose.

The entrance procession is accompanied either by the entrance chant, which can be said or sung (a preference for singing). The entrance chants are provided in the Roman Missal, along with a tune to chant them. A suitable hymn may be sung instead of the chant. The hymn should reflect similar themes to the entrance chant or perhaps themes which emerge from the Scripture readings for the day or reflect the liturgical feast or season. It is not any song that the choir happen to know or like. When we sing this song, it already begins the process of focusing our minds and hearts on the aspect of the Easter mystery we are celebrating today. It is a way of gathering our collective thoughts and it unifies us through our singing of the hymn with a robust and full voice. (This is not the time for our quiet voice.)

At the head of the procession is Christ not in person but symbolised in the Processional Cross carried by a server or acolyte if there is no server. This is the One we follow, the crucified and risen One. How remarkable that an ancient instrument of torture and death is now the sign in which we glory. Every Mass celebrates the Paschal mystery; that Christ died for our sins and on the third day he was raised to life, and, because of that, new life is possible for us. Jesus once said to his followers, 'Take up your cross and follow me'. How do we do that in our daily living?

There is one thing that can proceed the cross and this is the thurible, the container in which the incense is burned. It can be used at every Mass. When it is used, and it should be, at least every Sunday Mass, the incense reminds us – as it wafts over us – that we are the holy and priestly people who have come to offer the sacrifice of the Mass. It is a reminder of the incense that burns before the heavenly altar as described in the Book of Revelation. The smoke joins us to that heavenly community through sharing in the same olfactory and visual experience.

Altar servers and acolytes come after the cross. They are lay people like most of the assembly, and are in white robes (alb). The white robe is a symbol of baptism and also recalls the white-robed community assembled in the heavenly vision in the Book of Revelation. The alb is a sign of your own baptism and of the fact that you gather here and participate in this ritual because you are part of this white-robed community.

If the deacon is carrying the Evangeliary (Book of Gospels), he will process in ahead of the other deacons or presbyters and bishop. He will carry the Book slightly elevated and, without bowing to the altar, he will proceed directly up to the altar and 'enthrone' the Book of Gospels on it. The Gospel is the sign of Christ among us in his word. During the liturgy, we always have special signs that accompany the Gospel because it is so intimately associated with the words and deed of Jesus. Enthroning the Book joins together two primary symbols of Jesus' presence – Gospel and Altar.

The other ministers, including the one who presides, follow behind in the procession. It is important that they come last because it highlights that they too are followers of Jesus, disciples, also making their way to the Kingdom. There is no hierarchy of holiness in the Church; all are called to one and the same holiness. All are called to be transformed by the grace of Christ. The Bishop of Rome (Pope) may have the honorific title of Your Holiness, but it is more of an expression of hope than a statement of an achievement. We hope that the man God has chosen is striving for holiness. The woman sitting in a church in

Africa with a dirt floor, who may be illiterate and who does not know much about theology and doctrine, may be the holiest person in the Church, for all we know. What we do know is that she and the Pope are on the same pilgrim journey and trying to follow the same Lord Jesus Christ.

We are a pilgrim people. We are companions on a journey. Together, we are disciples of Christ, making our way along the road with him. The entrance procession can draw us into the deeper reality of that and pose questions for us. Have we made the cross our sign of faith, hope and love? Do we allow ourselves to be led by Jesus in our daily living or is it just a fleeting experience at Mass? Can we truthfully say that we have taken up our cross and that we follow him?

9

Singing

Our daughter loves choral music and has been in a choir from kindergarten all the way through to high school and for a few years after school too. A number of these choirs have been related to Lutheran schools or Anglican parishes. As a result, my wife and I have had wonderful experiences of choral performances in a variety of settings, concert halls, school halls and churches. I have also had a lot of opportunity to attend worship with Protestant Christians because I have been involved in a variety of ecumenical (church unity) projects and groups. I have had a lot of exposure to singing in Protestant Churches so I fully understand the choir master's sense of humour in the following story.

One of the choirs our daughter belonged to would host an annual carol service in the weeks leading up to Christmas. The more elaborate pieces would be performed by the choir alone but the audience would be invited to sing with some of the more well-known Advent and Christmas hymns. The venue would rotate among churches in the city. One year, the Catholic cathedral was hosting and the choir master explained that there would be opportunities for the audience to participate in the singing and then he joked, 'We may be in a Catholic cathedral but, when we sing, could we sing like we are Protestants?' It is true. It is an exceedingly rare thing to find a Catholic parish in Australia where the congregation sings with full voice. A local Protestant congregation of sixty can sing more lustily than a Catholic congregation of several hundred. I know we have different historical traditions of worship that may have contributed to this and perhaps it's our musical repertoire, but I do wish Catholics would sing.

Music and singing are central to Catholic worship. As with trying to understand all things about the Mass, the General Instruction on the Roman Missal (GIRM) should be consulted and there are other national and international documents that help to explain the role of music in the liturgy too. Here I will touch on just a few things. These are things which are good for you to understand so as to assist you to pray the Mass. If you how music fits into the Mass, you might appreciate it more and sing with greater enjoyment.

If your parish has musicians and choristers or at least some who can lead the singing, they should be encouraged to share their gifts and also to learn from GIRM about music in the Mass. Let's proceed working on these two assumptions – that they are present and aware of requirements. The first priority in singing are the parts of the Mass not hymns. If possible, the presbyter or bishop should sing (chant) rather than speak the words of the Mass. The deacon and people should chant or sing the responses. Chant and other music settings are provided for most texts of the Mass. There are even chant texts for the Gospel, which the deacon could use. When musicians choose settings, make as a priority setting in a mid-range key and with a regular and predictable rhythm so that most people can easily sing along. If your parish only sings the parts of the Mass and no hymns that would be enough.

It is helpful for worship if parishes use a number of settings for the parts of the Mass. There should be one setting used for Ordinary time, one for Easter (Paschal) season and one used in both Lent and Advent. Using one for a number of weeks helps people become more familiar with it and increases confidence in singing. It also helps to clearly mark off the movements of the liturgical year.

The choice of hymns is dictated by the part of the Mass being celebrated and the liturgical season or feast day being celebrated. The wishes and tastes of the presbyter or musicians are not elements that shape musical choices. Hymns are really only required for the entrance and during the rite of distribution of Holy Communion. It is suitable to have a hymn during the procession and preparation of gifts but music without singing could also be used at that time.

As with Mass settings, hymns that all will sing should also be chosen that are in a mid-range key and have a regular rhythm. It is recommended that a parish have a small set of hymns that are unique to each season, Ordinary time, Easter, Lent and Advent.

The purpose of the entrance hymn is to gather the hearts and minds of the congregation around the Mass we are celebrating today, including hymns that reflect aspects of the readings for the day. Suggestions for entrance hymns might also come from the movable texts of the Mass, i.e., the collect (opening prayer), prayer over the gifts, preface or prayer after communion. The choice will also reflect the action occurring at the time e.g. a procession, the music would be of the kind of tempo that will provide a satisfactory movement. A slow and meditative hymn or one that is overly brisk would not work.

Communion hymns commence as soon as the presider commences his communion and conclude after the last person has received communion. The general principle of choosing hymns that people can sing applies. What is to be sung is determined by what we are doing. We are receiving communion and deepening our communion with God and each other. All the hymns are about communion and nothing else. We do not sing hymns that will take our hearts and minds off this important procession and rite of receiving communion. We do not sing 'How Great Thou Art', 'Make Me a Channel of Your Peace', or 'City of God' and many other worthy hymns during communion. If it is not a hymn about communion, then it is not a hymn to accompany the rite of communion.

There is one hymn that is optional in the Roman or Latin Rite Mass, and another one that is not present at all but which frequently makes an appearance. After communion, there is the option of a period of silence or a hymn. Themes of communion and thanksgiving are suitable for this optional hymn. There is no recessional hymn. It is highly probable that you have sung one. It is simply not part of the liturgy but has become a practice from which few can seem to retreat.

Singing unites the congregation in a way that speaking does not. What we have known liturgically and spiritually for centuries has been demonstrated by modern neuroscience. Singing promotes the release of the kind of hormones that promote group bonding and a sense of solidarity. Singing also adds beauty to worship and allows musicians and composers to share the many gifts that God has supplied. A quote attributed to St Augustine is worth keeping in mind, 'Those who sings once, pray twice'.

10

Silence

Silence is a language all of its own. We know the awkward silence that follows a bad or tasteless joke shared at a gathering. We know the shocked silence when some seemingly incomprehensible news is delivered to us. Some of us know the beauty of silence shared when sitting with the person we most love and we watch a beautiful sunset and share the moment without words. Some have felt the silence of anxiety in a large house when we are all alone and in which every small sound seems to be magnified. In other words, silence is not without content and meaning.

At Mass, there are moments for silence and we can find the content and meaning of these silences if we are attentive to them. We can be enriched by the silence in the Mass. Immediately before Mass commences, it is good to have some time in silence to become aware of the Holy Presence of God and the holy presence of the holy Church gathered with me for this liturgy. A few moments of attentive recollection can help us centre on our purpose for being here and to unite our personal intentions with the intentions of the whole Church. Sometimes only a few seconds of this recollection time is available to parents with small children but some seconds are better than none.

Immediately after the opening prayer (collect) and before the Liturgy of the Word (readings) commence, it is useful for the clergy and people to pause briefly in silence to prepare themselves to receive the word of God. The simple intention to be open to receiving the Word of God may be enough to fill this brief silence. After each reading, a brief pause to allow the clergy and people to savour a word of two from the Scripture portion just read can slow down the process enough for us to be more attentive to the readings.

After the homily, it is recommended that all sit in silence for a moment to contemplate the Scriptures that have been proclaimed. The purpose of the homily is to help the people receive the word of God. The primary focus of this silence should be on the Word and the homily may simply point us toward themes that help us meditate on the Scripture and to help us reflect on them. It should be a productive silence and one free from distractions.

After communion has been distributed and the communion antiphon or hymns have finished it is recommended that all sit in silence for a period again. This silence provides us with a moment that parallels the silence after the Liturgy of the Word. We have been fed from two tables; the table of the Word and the table of the Eucharist. Each requires a moment of silence for us to fully digest what we have received. When we serve a multi-course meal, we don't immediately finish one course and start on the next. We like a bit of space between courses to savour and digest. This helps us appreciate the flavour of each course and the contribution of each to the whole of the meal.

In the Book of Kings, the Prophet Elijah waits to hear God. First, there is a mighty earthquake, but God is not in the earthquake. Next, there is strong wind, strong enough to split rocks! God is not in that mighty wind. Finally, there is a quiet and gentle breeze and Elijah goes out and there he encounters God in that gentle silence.

Silence in the liturgy allows us to know the presence of God in the gentleness of sitting still, away from the movement and sound of processions, songs and readings. We enter the silence and meet God in the quiet inner sanctuary that is our conscience. There we stand before God in awe. God, who sees into the heart, can meet us in this inner place and speak to us a word that we need to hear. Perhaps this word is just for me to hear and to take into my life.

When we look at cows in the field, when they are not mooing, they are chewing. They ruminate on the grass and take their time to chew and process it. It is a slower process of digestion than ours. We chew rather efficiently and swallow. Perhaps we need to learn from the cows the art of rumination. We can sit in silence for a while and chew over the word carefully and slowly before we begin to swallow it and before we even begin to digest its meaning. We cease our 'mooing'- the singing, talking and reading and instead keep on 'chewing'. Silence allows is to savour the word of God. Silence allows us to ponder all these things in our heart.

During the week, it is good to make time to ruminate on the Scriptures and to digest their meaning more fully. It is good to find a few moments for sacred silence outside of the Mass. When we make this a regular habit, we soon learn of the rich content and meaning of sacred silence.

Silence is an important element of the liturgy. It is not dead time, while we wait for the next thing to happen. Silence is 'something happening' if we are well disposed to it. God, who is as gentle as silence, can be heard speaking in this silence if we listen with the ear of the heart.

11

Bells and smells

I remember attending Mass at Notre Dame Cathedral in Paris on the Feast of Epiphany. In France, as in many other European nations, it is a public holiday and the day on which families gather to exchange gifts, recalling the Magi who brought gifts to Jesus. There was a large crowd at Mass as well as tourists wandering around the church. I was struck by how much smoke was produced by the thurible (the brass container in which the incense is burned) as the procession made its way toward the altar. Great clouds of incense rose up and created beautiful patterns as shafts of light passed through the clouds and the perfume was intoxicating. The incense was used at every part indicated in the Mass and with equal volumes of sweet-smelling clouds. The effects of the clouds of smoke and the perfume created an other-worldly atmosphere and seemed to transport us to heaven.

Catholic Mass is a very incarnational and spiritual celebration. By incarnational, I mean that we use all of the senses of the body to pray the Mass – sight, sound, touch, taste and smell. We also pray with the movement of our bodies, kneeling, sitting, standing, crossing ourselves, extending hands over gifts etc. to make the incarnational dimension even deeper. Spiritual too, because we sacramentalise these senses by using them to experience a deeper spiritual and mystical reality.

Before the reforms of the Mass after Vatican II, which took us back to the Mass closest to the original style of celebration, there were two forms of the Mass. One was called the low Mass and the other the high Mass. The distinction between the two was largely about more embellished rituals and chanting and the use of incense. After the Council, this distinction was abolished and we had one form of the ordinary form of the Traditional Latin Mass[4] (Paul VI) which we celebrate every Sunday and weekday in parishes across the world.

In the reforms of Vatican II, the use of incense was retained and its use extended to all Masses. In Australia at the time, when the use of incense was made more available, many parishes ceased to use it altogether except for special times like Easter and, of course, at funerals. Because of this restricted use, many Catholics incorrectly

---

4 The Mass we have from the Second Vatican Council is the ordinary traditional Latin Mass. It comes to us from the tradition and is written in Latin. Some incorrectly use the term exclusively for the extraordinary form of the Mass of the Roman Rite which preceded this revised form.

associate incense with the funeral and we are deprived of the enrichment incense provides to our praying through incorporation of a richer sense of smell and sight.

At every Mass, incense can be used (and should be used, in my view, at least on Sundays) in all of the places indicated. These places are at the commencement of Mass, at the gospel, during the preparation of gifts and, optionally, during the Eucharistic prayer.

At the commencement of Mass, the incense – which should burn with plentiful and visible smoke – leads the procession. The incense is placed in the thurible and blessed by the one presiding. The incense transforms the place from the realm of the ordinary to gather our hearts and minds with the communion of the whole Church on earth and in heaven. The sweet-smelling smoke drifts through the people and reminds us that this is the priestly people, the holy nation who are gathered to offer the Mass as an expression of this priestly dignity. It is a reminder that Christ is truly present in the assembly, his Body the Church.

Once the procession reaches the altar, the presider and deacon – after reverencing the altar with a kiss – form a procession, circle the altar and incense it. The altar is a sanctified space, which is both Christ himself and the sacrifice that is be offered. The cross, and – if it is the Easter season – the Paschal Candle are also incensed. The same smoke joins the people to the symbols so sanctified by the incense and makes them one with the sacred objects. They are united with the altar and cross and Paschal Candle.

When the alleluia chant begins for the Procession of the Gospel, the priest blesses the incense and the deacon who will proclaim the Gospel. We will look at how the incense is used during the Gospel in another section.

After the gifts have been prepared and before the Eucharistic Prayer, the presider and deacon once again form a procession. The priest first incenses the gifts placed on the altar and then once more they circle the altar. After that, the deacon incenses the presider because he acts in the person of Christ, Head of the Church. He exercises his priesthood at this moment in a way that is different from that of deacon and lay people. (If there are concelebrating bishops and presbyters, he will incense them next.)

Next, the deacon goes to the people and all rise and bow. He incenses the people to remind them that they are also exercising their priestly ministry as the Body of Christ, and to join the priest, altar and gifts together. The smoke helps to produce the unity between them. The symbolism is clearer in the Eastern Catholic Churches because the deacon comes down and walks among the people so that the incense wafts around the whole assembly.

There is an option to use incense during the Eucharistic Prayer. A server or acolyte kneels at the foot of the altar and swings the thurible during the prayer and, at the elevation of the host and then the chalice, it is raised and swung three times. Bells may also be rung during the elevation of host and chalice. The essential purpose of the bells is to draw our attention to the consecrated elements.

When we see and smell the incense, we could recall the words of the Psalmist, 'O God, I am calling to you, hurry to me, listen to the sound of my voice when I call to you. May my prayer be like incense in your presence' (Psalm 141:1-2).

12

Vestments

Catholic, Orthodox and some Protestant communities retain the use of vestments for lay people and clergy. Like everything that happens in Catholic liturgy, it is always about the whole assembly not just those who happen to be wearing vestments.

The alb is the most basic liturgical vestment. Alb means white. This long white robe is worn by altar servers, acolytes, deacons, presbyters and bishops. If it is a loose style, it may be tied with a rope belt called a cincture, but, if it is fitted, the cincture is not required. An alb is the robe of baptism and is a symbol that the assembly is not like any ordinary crowd of people like you might find at a football match or a concert hall. These are the priestly people, the holy nation. This is the white robed army assembled around the throne of God and the Lamb in the Book of Revelation (Revelation 7:9). When we see the alb, we should recall that it is a symbol to remind us of our baptism and who we are. The alb should remind us of the words of St Paul, 'I have been crucified with Christ and yet I am alive, and yet it is no longer I, but Christ living in me. The life I now live in the body, I live by faith in the Son of God, who loved me and gave himself for me' (Galatians 2:20).

Bishops, deacons and presbyters wear a stole over the alb. The stole is a band of cloth like a big scarf. A deacon wears his stole over the left shoulder and it is gathered at the right hip. A presbyter or bishop wears his stole around his neck and it hangs down either side of his chest. The stole is a sign of the office or function he holds within the community. Stoles come in colours matching the liturgical season and may be decorated with images and symbols taken from nature, the life of Christ or symbols like crosses.

Over the alb and stole, the deacon wears a vestment called a dalmatic. This is a long tunic with sleeves. It will be in the same colours as the stole and may also be decorated in similar ways. This is an ancient vestment and was originally part of the uniform of magistrates, ambassadors and other officials of the Roman Empire. This is because the ancient Greek word *diaconos*, from which we get our word deacon, meant someone of some significance who had been given a commission or task to perform on behalf of another. The deacon receives a commission to serve the ministry of the bishop in the diocese in which he is ordained. In early iconography, Jesus is frequently depicted in a dalmatic because he is the *diaconos* of God. St Ignatius of Antioch speaks of the deacon as the icon of Christ standing in the midst of the community.

Presbyters and bishops wear a chasuble over the alb and stole. The chasuble is a cape-like garment with no sleeves. It will be in the same colours as the dalmatic and it too may be decorated with symbols and images. The origins of the chasuble are less clear. It may have come from practices in Roman pre-Christian religion as part of priestly vesture.

There are a number of liturgical colours that tell us which season we are in and also something of the meaning of the season for us. Purple is used in Advent and Lent and both are seasons of preparation. The year begins with the season of Advent. This is a colour of penance and sorrow and so it tells us that Advent is a season of penance in preparation for the season of Christmas. It is not as strict a penitential season as Lent and for this reason, in some churches, the Advent vestments are not as dark purple as the Lent ones. Each time we see the purple vestments, we might pray that God will help us prepare our hearts to celebrate nativity or Pascha (Easter) with sincerity and deep effects.

Green is the colour of Ordinary Time. It is a colour of hope and persistence. We might recall the evergreen trees that survive through winter with their green foliage intact. We might also recall the image from scripture of the trees planted by the riverside that always remain fresh and strong. Christ is the water of life and we are planted close to him and receive life from him. We might recall the words of the Prophet Jeremiah speaking about those who trust in God, 'They will be like a tree planted by the waterside that thrusts its roots to the stream: when heat comes, it has nothing to fear; its foliage always stays green. Untroubled in a year of drought it never stops bearing fruit' (Jeremiah 17:8).

White is the colour for the seasons of Christmas and Easter (Pascha). Gold can also be used. White is a colour of joy and celebration. It is the colour of our baptism. We were baptised into the death and resurrection of Christ and now our life is with him. In the incarnation which we celebrate at the Feast of Nativity (Christmas), God comes among us as one like us in all things (consubstantial) except sin, in order that we can be taken up into his life and be transformed into the image of the Son. In the festival of Easter, we enter into the life of Christ through his dying and rising which we experienced in baptism. Perhaps when we see the white vestments we might pray; 'Lord Jesus, with you I will die and rise again'. In this prayer, we recognise our faults and failings but also our desire to die to them in order to rise with Christ to fullness of life.

Vestments engage our sense of sight. The vestments should be simple but beautiful or have the quality of noble simplicity. Their beauty should lift up our hearts to higher things. Vestments also have the advantage of de-centring the minister. When they wear vestments, it is no longer I, an Anthony or a Peter, who is ministering but the office of deacon or presbyter or bishop that is ministering. It is no longer about me but about who and what I am before God and this community. Vestments tell a bigger story and that story should never be about making the one wearing them the centre of that story.

13

Praying with our body

A non-Catholic friend who accompanied me to Mass a few times said to me that all of this standing and sitting and kneeling was like a form of Catholic aerobic exercise. Although he was only joking, it did make me recognise how much we use our bodies to pray. There is a lot of physical movement of our whole body or parts of our body by the congregation and the clergy. We are so used to it that perhaps we take some of it for granted and it takes an outsider to bring it to our attention.

As soon as we enter the church, we make the sign of the cross on our bodies. We bow or genuflect toward the altar or else the tabernacle if it is in the sanctuary. We stand for the entrance procession and for the introductory rites of the Mass. Then we sit to hear the readings, except the Gospel, when we stand again and then we sit for the homily. Then we stand again to profess our faith and to offer prayers for the Church and the world.

We sit for the presentation of gifts and stand for the start of the dialogue before the Eucharistic Prayer and then we kneel (although not in all countries) for the Eucharist prayer, stand to pray the Lord's Prayer and exchange the peace, and after the Lamb of God, we kneel again.

At communion time, we begin a procession, a Eucharistic procession, to receive Holy Communion and return to our seats. Then we may sit or kneel and we sing while all take communion. After communion, we all sit in silence together for a time of prayer and meditation. Then we stand again for the Prayer after Communion. We might sit for announcements and then stand again for the blessing and then form another procession while we leave the church to go on mission.

We have not only made the sign of the cross as we entered but also to commence the Mass, along with the presider and the people. We made the sign of the cross before the reading of the Gospel on our forehead, lips and across our heart. We make the sign of the cross at the end as we receive the blessing at the end of Mass.

We reach across and shake the hands of members (pre-COVID) of the assembly at the exchange of peace. We also extended our hand to receive communion. In Australia, we briefly bowed before we approached the communion minister.

At various times, the deacon and presbyter or bishop made some gestures that are related to their task in the Mass. They have opened wide their arms to announce the presence of the Lord. They have made the sign of the cross in the same way as the people at the start of Mass but the presider makes the sign of the cross over the people at the end. They have bowed to the altar, kissed the altar, walked around the altar, kissed the Book of Gospels or lectionary after proclaiming the Gospel. The priest at the Eucharistic Prayer raises his hands for most of the prayer but holds his hands over the gifts when he calls down the Holy Spirit to consecrate and make Holy the bread and wine so that it will become the Body and Blood of our Lord Jesus Christ. He makes the sign of the cross over the bread and wine. He breaks the bread, sometimes assisted by the deacon, and places a small fragment of it into the chalice. He lifts up the bread and wine to show the people and, if there is a deacon present (but not another priest), the deacon will take the cup and lift it while the priest lifts up the host.

There is no time here to look at the meaning of each gesture but just a few general principles. As far as possible, all the people should perform the same gestures in the same way and at the same time. For example, all should stand to receive communion and preferably in the hand (as that is the longest tradition in the Church) rather than some kneeling to receive or kneel before receiving instead of the bow. This is because we want to visibly demonstrate our unity and communion through our gestures. Mass is not a time for private devotions or practice; this is the Body of Christ at prayer, our public prayer. We need to be in time with or in step with each other. It is like going to a dance in a local hall and the band is playing a waltz; the steps that go with it, and the one your partner has already commenced is a waltz. This is not time for you to start a tango or the twist. When you go to the dance with your dance partner and at that dance hall, they play mostly waltz music, you should expect to do the waltz and not a dance more suited to rock or pop music. So, the first principle is to be in step with the assembly.

The second principle is to recall that God created us as spirited-bodies. God comes to save us body and soul, not only our souls. There is no disembodied salvation and one day we shall rise again and be known through the particularities of our bodies. All people are created in the image and likeness of God. In Christ, God came among us as one of us (consubstantial with us) and in doing so made us a new creation through baptism so that we might wear the image of the New Adam, Jesus. We have become part of the Body of Christ, and it is his body that makes these gestures – in, through and with us in the Holy Spirit. Perhaps, we should become more mindful of the gestures and the way the word takes flesh in us through them.

14

Getting started

We have already reflected on some of the aspects of getting started at Mass, with the way we individually enter and also the rite of entry with the procession and also the purpose of the hymn that we sing to commence the Mass. From the moment the entrance hymn or chant commences, we are being gathered into one. We are forming ourselves as the priestly people and leaving behind some of individual concerns and devotions and deepening the experience of becoming one Body in Christ. This is as true of the deacon and presbyter as it is of the congregation.

We adopt a common posture by standing for the entrance, not as a mark of respect to the clergy, but to literally stand up and be counted. We announce our presence as the priestly people gathered here to offer the sacrifice of the Mass. The standing is a sign of our unity. Of course, if you are frail and unable to stand or have some physical restrictions on standing, you are still gathered and numbered among the faithful. Notice that everyone. clergy and laity, adopt the same posture of standing.

When the entrance song is completed, all mark their bodies with the sign of the cross. The clergy and laity make the sign in the same way. Only at the end of Mass does the presider trace the sign of the cross in the air and over the people. Next, we start a dialogue with each other that will continue throughout Mass. The Church are those people whose unity springs from the unity of the Father, Son and Holy Spirit. When we make the sign of the cross together at this point in the Mass, we are acknowledging that our unity does not result from our own decision, it is a gift, a participation in Trinitarian communion. This a communion that we entered through baptism. In baptism, we were immersed into the death and resurrection of Jesus and are united with him.

The presider, if he is a presbyter, will say, 'The Lord be with you.', if the presider is a bishop he will say, 'Peace be with you'. The people respond, 'And with your spirit'. Both phrases from the presider announce the presence of the Lord Jesus among us. It is he who is the true presider and true priest of the sacrifice of the Mass. The bishop uses the words Jesus spoke to the disciples in the appearance stories after his resurrection. A bishop is a kind of icon of Christ present in the community and is the head of the local Church. A sign of Christ who is the Head of his Body the Church. Neither the presbyter nor bishop is Christ and so the people respond that they wish the presence of the Risen Lord to be with the presider too. We have recently returned to the literal translation of the response of the people. It has a richer meaning that the former, 'And also with you'. To say 'with your spirit' means to indicate that Jesus is present to your deepest, most essential core or essence of your being. That is where each of us encounters the Risen Lord.

Sometimes a presider is tempted to start another dialogue – a dialogue of hello and welcome. Actually, there are very few times that such a thing should ever happen and not just because it is not a part of the Mass, because it misses the point of the introductory rites. The times when the dialogue of welcome could occur – and when it does it should be brief and respectful of the Mass – may be at a funeral Mass, a Mass for a special occasion when there may be many non-Catholics present, or perhaps at Easter and Christmas when there are visitors or Catholics who only come at these times. A word of welcome may be very appropriate and pastorally sensitive.

The introductory rite is not a time for the presider to ask visitors to identify themselves and where they have come from or to have a competition about who has travelled the furthest to be here today. It is not a time for the presider to ask all the children twelve or under to stand on their seat so that the congregation can applaud their presence. It is not a time for the presider to ask who is celebrating a birthday or anniversary this week and have to congregation applaud them. All of these things and more I have experienced at Mass.

This entrance, this sign of the cross, this announcing of the presence of the Lord, has the purpose of reminding us about the source of our unity. We are called and gathered by the Lord. We are not a Jesus fan club, we are not members of a group like one can be a member of a sports club, an arts group or a political party which one pays to join as a member. We are members of the Body of Christ in the sense that arms and legs are part of a body. We are members of Christ and therefore of one another.

When we stand, sign ourselves, announce the presence of the Lord, we recall that ultimately, we are here because we have a vocation to be Church. We are the called ones. We are called by Christ, through the Holy Spirit, into the inner sanctum, the Holy of Holies, to stand in the presence of God. When we stand, we put on our priesthood and we stand with the whole company of the Church in heaven and earth. These simple gestures, movements and words are filled with deep and rich meaning. God finds us worthy to stand in His presence and serve Him.[5] We need some sense of the honour God bestows on us in calling each woman and man gathered at Mass to fulfil a priestly vocation. We are not worthy because of our own merits but because the grace of Christ claimed us at baptism. We know our own weakness and even sinfulness but we need to know also that God chooses us for this priesthood and makes a holy people. All of this is profound truth, and we are just getting started in the Mass.

---

5 God is not a male but by tradition, and because Jesus calls God Father, we use masculine pronouns. I capitalise these to indicate that I am not speaking of a male. Jesus is a male and so I do use lower case he and him when I refer to him.

15

The Father is running to us

There was a man who would complain to the presbyter after every Mass. He would have a complaint about how someone was dressed inappropriately, or how some parents allowed their children to behave, or complain about the young people who would arrive for Mass late and with alcohol on their breath and how they must have just come from the pub down the road. There were also complaints about the homily and the singing and... well, complaints about a lot of things. One day, he said to the presbyter, 'Father, I just don't think I can keep coming here anymore. I am going to have to find another parish'. The presbyter replied, 'I will be sad to see you go. You have been part of this parish family for a long time. You do know that when find your new parish, it won't be perfect anymore, once you have arrived'.

After we exchange the greeting, we are invited to prepare ourselves (this is the Penitential Act) to celebrate the sacred mysteries. That preparation is done by confessing sin and asking forgiveness. We know that we are God's holy people but we also know that we are not God's perfect people. Neither the clergy nor the laity are free from sin and failings and the things that make it difficult for us to truly witness to the Gospel in a credible display of Christian living. Even though we might strive for perfection and true holiness and we fall short, the effectiveness of the celebration of the sacred mysteries is not impaired. It is Christ working in and through us that is the cause of the effectiveness of the sacraments. God was smart enough to know that the effectiveness of the sacraments could not rest on the holiness or worthiness of the minister and the Church that celebrates them.

Saints and sinners gather with you at Mass most Sundays. It is not for you to know which is which, but God does. It has always been thus. That is why Jesus tells the story of the wheat and the darnel (Matthew 13:24-30). A farmer sows some wheat in his field, but an enemy comes and sows darnel in the field with the wheat when no one is looking. As the two plants grow, they resemble each other very closely and of course they are intermingled. When he is asked by the farm hands if they should pull them out, the farmer says no. There is a risk that wheat will be lost with the weeds. He says when the harvest comes and the ears of grain are clearer to distinguish, we will separate them and burn the weeds in a fire. Jesus tells us this story to remind us that wheat and weeds grow in the field that is the Church. On the Day of Judgment, they will be separated.

This is not an argument for complacency in the spiritual life or for acceptance of some fatalistic outcome. We are each called to holiness and called to the same holiness which is a communion with the Holy Trinity. It is no different if you are a Pope, some other bishop, a presbyter a Religious Sister or Brother, a deacon or a lay person. We are meant to strive and to try and grow with the grace of Christ toward a robust Christian witness in every aspect of our lives. To know that there are weeds among the wheat is simply to know the reality that God loves this fractured and imperfect world – not some idealised version of what the world should be. God knows what life could be and calls us to share in that vision and live the kind of life consistent with that vision in this imperfect world.

There are a number of ways that we can prepare ourselves to celebrate the sacred mysteries. We can say or chant the *Kyrie eleison* (Lord, have mercy), say or chant one of the responsorial style versions of the Kyrie, or recite the general confession, 'I confess to Almighty God...' and sometimes through a rite of sprinkling with water, especially during the Easter season. No matter what version is used, as soon as the prayer or chant concludes, and without any pause, the presider will pray, 'May almighty God have mercy on us, forgive us our sins and bring us to everlasting life'. He includes himself in this prayer.

It seems significant to me that there is no gap between the ending of the prayer asking forgiveness and the prayer of absolution. It reminds me of the son (sometimes referred to as the prodigal son) who has spent his inheritance on wild living and who now returns to his father's house (Luke 15:11-32). On the way to the father, he is rehearsing his confession but he does not have time to get the words out before his father expresses his love and gives his absolution.

I think it would help us pray the penitential act more deeply if we imagine that we are this wayward son or daughter and that our prayer, as we prepare ourselves to celebrate the sacred mysteries (mystery means sacrament), is like the rehearsed prayer of the child returning. In the Gospel story, while the child is a long way off, the father runs to him and embraces him. He loves him and forgives him. That is what God is doing for us during the penitential act. He is running toward us as soon as He begins to hear our rehearsed prayer seeking forgiveness and we have barely got the last word from our lips when He embraces each daughter and son present in the assembly with the words, 'I have mercy on you, I forgive your sins and I am leading you to everlasting life. Come and join the banquet I have prepared for you'. Accept that embrace as you hear the words of absolution at the conclusion of the Penitential Act.

16

Lord, have mercy

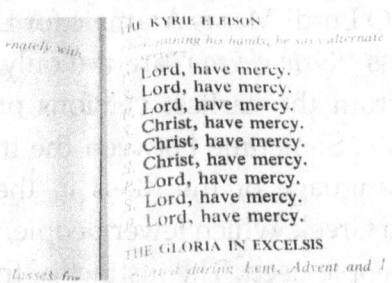

R ecently, I was in a supermarket doing my normal grocery shopping in one of those shops where they always have background music interspersed with the occasional advertisement or the jingle associated with their brand. While I was working my way through the fruit and vegetable section, a song from the 1980s, 'Kyrie' by Mr Mister (a pop band from the USA) began to play. In every chorus. the phrase *Kyrie eleison* (Lord have mercy) repeats several times. In the final stanza the band just kept repeating *Kyrie eleison* almost in a litany style. I wondered how many of my fellow shoppers recognised the Greek phrase 'Lord, have mercy' or knew of its significance in the liturgy of both Catholic and Orthodox Christians.

There are a lot of Greek words in the Christian vocabulary, words such as baptism, catechumen and eucharist. The Second Testament was written in a language called Koine Greek. The First Testament used by the first Christians was the Greek version (Septuagint version) because most of them were Greek-speaking people. *Kyrie*, Lord, is one of the earliest titles assigned to Jesus by the early Church, perhaps within a short time after the resurrection. We know this because its Aramaic version survives in the Second Testament in the phrase, *'Maran na'tha'*, Come O Lord! *Mar* is Aramaic for Lord.

In the Mass *'Kyrie eleison'* are the only Greek words that remain from the earliest versions of the Mass in the Roman Rite. Sometime between the third and sixth century the language of the Mass in the Roman Rite switched from Greek, which fewer people, used to Latin, which most people used. The instinct of the Church has been to pray in the language of the people. Even the Council of Trent in the sixteenth century recognised that Latin had ceased to function as a living language for most people and allowed that the Mass could be celebrated in any language provided that people did not say that they thought Mass celebrated in Latin was not valid. From the Second Vatican Council (1962-65), permission was given to celebrate Mass in a combination of the local language and Latin or just the local language.

When we pray *Kyrie eleison* by singing or saying it, we are taking ourselves back to the earliest generations of Christians in Rome, and to much of the ancient world which spoke Greek. The language connects us with them across time into a communion of prayer. It connects us also with the language of the Bible which the first Christians used. We still use the Greek Bible today, although we hear it in our own language because of the expertise of translators. It is worth savouring the words themselves and listening to their sound so that we can call to mind our foremothers and forefathers in the Christian faith.

Praying the words also takes us into the Gospels. We can imagine that we are like the man born blind who calls out, 'Jesus, son of David, have mercy on me!' (Mark 10:47-52)

> Then they came to Jericho. As Jesus and his disciples, together with a large crowd, were leaving the city, a blind man, Bartimaeus (which means 'son of Timaeus'), was sitting by the roadside begging. When he heard that it was Jesus of Nazareth, he began to shout, 'Jesus, Son of David, have mercy on me!' Many rebuked him and told him to be quiet, but he shouted all the more, 'Son of David, have mercy on me!' Jesus stopped and said, 'Call him'. So they called to the blind man, 'Cheer up! On your feet! He's calling you'. Throwing his cloak aside, he jumped to his feet and came to Jesus. 'What do you want me to do for you?' Jesus asked him. The blind man said, 'Rabbi, I want to see'. 'Go', said Jesus, 'your faith has healed you'. Immediately he received his sight and followed Jesus along the road. (*New International Version*)

As soon as Bartimaeus hears that it is Jesus, he calls out. He hears and believes; he has not yet seen. In that way he is like us. Notice how at first the disciples get in the way of the relationship between Bartimaeus and Jesus. I wonder how often we let others get in our way. Do we see the weakness in individual members of the

Church or the Church in general and let that keep us from our relationship with Christ? On the other hand, is the behaviour of some in the Church so scandalous that it causes us to stumble along the way and makes it hard for us to remain connected to the Body of Christ.

Notice that Jesus does not call the man directly to himself. He instructs his disciples who had previously been the barrier to his inclusion to go and issue the invitation. That is, Jesus invites us to have a change of heart, a conversion, so that we can play a part in the calling and the healing of others. Jesus uses this as a moment for our further instruction to learn how wide is the scope of Divine love.

See with how much energy and passion Bartimaeus responds to the call, throwing his cloak aside and running. Some of the wise women and men of the early Church saw in his behaviour an image of baptism. The setting aside of the old self and the alacrity of the response to the Gospel (Good News). Running in the way of the Gospel.

Jesus does not presume to know what the man wants or needs. Jesus enters into dialogue with him, 'What do you want me to do for you?' Jesus enters into dialogue with us. What do we say to him about the sins we need forgiven, when we call to mind our sins? What healing do we need? When we name our faults and sins immediately, we hear Jesus say, 'your faith has healed you'. We can trust that our sins are forgiven when we pray *Kyrie eleison*, Lord, have mercy.

17

Forgiveness and community

We have already noted that when we participate in Mass, we are not participating in Mass as isolated individuals. We gather as the Church, the Body of Christ. We have also noted that the 'we' of the Mass includes all who are gathered with me in the church, all Catholics throughout the world now, and the whole company of heaven, the angels and saints. We matter to each other and we have impacts on each other.

As I write this, the whole world is grappling with a pandemic. If there is one thing we have learned from trying to deal with this crisis, it will be that what each of us does can have an impact on others. We are all connected. We have relied on each other to keep all of us safe by observing proper hygiene and spatial distancing. We have learned that although we put space between ourselves physically, we are intertwined and connected in society and are part of each other. Perhaps, we needed to relearn the lesson that what we do as individuals has an impact on the community.

One of the forms of the Penitential Act is to pray together a prayer known to us by its first Latin word, *Confiteor*, I confess. Twice in the prayer we acknowledge that we are part of a bigger group and that what we do as individuals has an impact on the whole. This is one of the few times we pray in our own name in the Mass. Normally, we use the plural 'we' but in this prayer we say 'I'.

We begin, 'I confess to almighty God and to you my brothers and sisters'. We need not only to let God know we have sinned but also those with whom we gather. We don't simply designate them as 'you who gather with me', as we used to say, 'and you here present'. Now we have returned to the original text and acknowledge that this is not the kind of crowd that may be present at a football match or cinema. The people I have gathered with are my sisters and my brothers.

We have been made sisters and brothers, not through biological connection or adoption, but through baptism. We are sons and daughters of God the Father because we have been baptised into and have become part of His Son, Jesus. We should dwell on these words and ponder them from time to time. Do we have a sense that this seemingly random group assembled here are my sisters and brothers? This is the first time in the Mass at which we acknowledge them as such. Interesting that we do so in the context of acknowledging our faults and failings. We are in effect saying, that 'I am not better than you, but

I am no worse than you either'. We are both capable of sin and failure.

After we own up to our sins in thought, word and deed, we address our sisters and brothers once more. We also address the wider group of sisters and brothers when we pray; 'therefore I ask blessed Mary ever-virgin, all the angels and saints'. That is very impressive company and a significant number of folks to whom we appeal for prayerful support. There is a vast number of saints throughout the ages and countless angels who we ask to pray with us. Again, it is worth pondering sometimes exactly whose help we are soliciting and asking to pray with us to overcome sin.

We ask our sisters and brothers, 'to pray for me to the Lord our God'. We are not praying to Mary and the saints but asking them to pray for us to God. We can only address our prayer to God even if we do so through the assistance of the angels and saints and our sisters and brothers. We are asking all of these others to intercede for us and to support us in overcoming sin. We acknowledge that we need each other and we acknowledge that we have to pray for one another. We are all in this together.

We do not go to God alone. We always have companions on the journey. My companions, my brothers and sisters, may be rich or poor, well-educated or not, well dressed or not, from a variety of nations and cultures and have many other things which set us apart. We are united in at least three things which we acknowledge in this form of the Penitential Act: we share a common baptism into

Christ, we are all sinners and, most importantly, we are all redeemed and forgiven sinners.

Take some time to ponder the connection between forgiveness and community. Our personal failures and faults have an impact on the whole Body of Christ. To the extent that each member of the Church is sinful, the holiness of the Church fails to shine through. Conversely, when we grow in holiness and capacity to live with the love and compassion with which Jesus lived, we let the light of the Gospel penetrate the darkness of the world. Our faults and failings have effects on my sisters and brothers in Christ and I need them to pray for me and for them to know that I am not perfect. I need to pray for them and I need to make room for their faults and failings, just as I hope that they will make room for me. We are, truly, all in this together.

18

Thought, word and deed

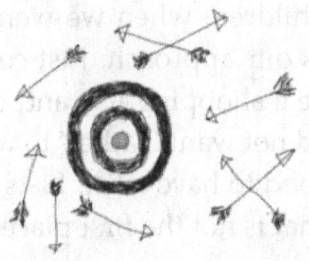

Staying with the Penitential Act and the Confiteor, let's have a short meditation on sin. In the Confiteor, we say that I have sinned 'in my thoughts and in my words, in what I have done and in what I have failed to do'. This a very comprehensive list of the how and where of sin and it is worth pondering this a little.

We should not be afraid of the word sin or back away from it or see it as an overly negative term. It is true that sometimes clergy may had put too much emphasis on sin and our failings, but let us not react by ignoring the reality because it may have seemed to us to be too heavily emphasised at one point. To ignore sin has real dangers for our full flourishing as human beings.

First, let us consider the word sin. In the Second Testament, the Greek word that is used for sin is *hamartia*. This is a word that comes from the sport of archery. *Hamartia* means to miss or to fall short of the mark or the target. The archer aims for the centre and when she misses the target, the one down the other end, keeping a score of the shots, calls out *hamartia*! It is an interesting word to choose for sin.

Sometimes when we think of sin, we think of a list of things we have done wrong as our first thought. Sometimes as children, when we went to confession at school, that was our approach. Just come up with a list of sins, a bit like a shopping list, and confess this to the priest. We would not want 'Father' to waste his morning. It was always good to have a list. Lists are good and can be helpful but that is not the first place to go to when we think of sin.

The image of the archer tells us more about the relationship of sin to what it is that what we are actually attempting to do in confessing it. Our aim, the target, is Christ Jesus. We aiming to be like Christ, to imitate his love and compassion. We believe that Jesus is one like the Father in all things and one like us in all things but sin. Jesus not only reveals what God is but reveals what fully human flourishing is like. He is the fullness of divinity and the fullness of humanity. Jesus loved with a human heart, and thought with a human mind and spoke with a human voice and therefore if he is capable of such great love in thought and word and deed, then so too are we. We cannot get to this fullness of life by our own efforts. Christianity is not a self-improvement society. We rely on grace from Christ to perfect our natures to become Christlike.

Another aspect of the archery image is that we cannot improve our aim alone. We stand at some distance from the target and cannot judge clearly for ourselves if we have to aim a little higher, lower, more to the left or more to the right. When learning the skill in the ancient world, the one calling out *hamartia* also had a flag to indicate a new coordinate for us and to help us improve our aim. We have these 'flags' now, they are called Scripture, Tradition, the teaching of the Church, the lives of the saints, the sacraments and so many other 'flags' to indicate how we can improve our aim.

Our real aim is to be more like Christ and, therefore, become more fully human. Not sinning is our indication that we are improving our aim but is not the final goal. This is where we come back to sinful attitudes or dispositions and then, below that are lists of particular sinful things. The Confiteor gives a useful matrix to guide an examination of our conscience. We can sin in our words, in our thoughts and in what we do and what we fail to do. It is worth stopping for five or ten minutes each night before we go to bed and checking out each part of this matrix.

When we look back over our day, did we use hurtful words? Did we hand on a rumour we had heard about someone? Did we share with someone else a fault or failing we noticed in someone but without any need to do so other than harming their reputation? Did we use coarse or vulgar speech when a better choice of words would have been as effective and not offensive? Did we use our words as a weapon to harm another or make them feel small and inadequate?

As we reflect over the day, how may we have fallen short of the mark with our thoughts? Did we think badly of another or take delight in their failings? Did we imagine doing things which we knew to be sinful, or imagine saying things which would be sinful? Did we let our mind wander towards thoughts of harm to another or using a person as an object of our own desires and satisfactions? Did we look at someone and fail to recognise their full dignity as a human being either through racist, sexist thoughts or because they were smelly and dirty, that made us make a negative judgment about them?

Deeds fall into two categories – the things we do that fall short of the mark because they harm me or others and the things that we ought to have done but failed to do. These are the things that we recognised at the time were good but did not follow through and do them. Where did our deeds fall short of the mark of being Christlike today? Did we see or hear someone being racist and fail to speak up against that and come to the defence of the person being denigrated? Did I take property from someone or deprive someone of their fair share because I was greedy and took more? Did I fail to curb my appetite when I ate or drank and my consumption was excessive?

Examining our conscience about our thoughts, words and deeds is a way of training to improve our aim so that we can become more like Christ and learn what it means to flourish fully as a human being and thereby know true and lasting happiness.

19

Glory to God

So much of the text of the Mass comes to us from Scripture. The first lines of the Gloria – 'Glory to God in the highest and on earth peace to people of good will' – come to us from the Gospel of Luke and the words the angels address to the shepherds as they announce the birth of Jesus. We sing the Gloria on most Sundays of the year but not the Sundays of Lent. When we sing or say these words, we are taken to that very moment when God comes among us, as one like us in all things but sin. God's Holy Presence among us in a way that no one expected.

The second stanza of the prayer is addressed to God the Father. We praise, bless, adore, glorify and give thanks to God. Notice the phase that follows – 'for your great glory'. This phrase, which comes from Scripture, and especially the word 'glory' used in this context, refers to God's Holy presence among us. This stanza relates to the first because we are giving praise, blessing, adoration and glorification to the Divine Presence among us. God is close to us and has come closer by sharing in our human life.

The next two stanzas are directed to Jesus and commences with six titles given to Jesus in the Scriptures. The first title is Lord or in Greek *Kyrios*. What is remarkable about this title is that in the First Testament it is used as a way of referring to God the Father in the Greek version of the First Testament (Septuagint). More remarkable still is that Christians began to apply this title to Jesus from the earliest stages of the emergence of the Christian community. So early that we find it contained in an Aramaic expression (the language spoken by Jesus and the apostles) in letters of Paul which are written in Greek. That is in the form of 'Mar' in the Aramaic expression *'mar a-natha'* or 'Come O Lord!' (1 Corinthians 16:22)

Christ is the second title. Christ (*Christos*) is the Greek form of the Aramaic and Hebrew words for Messiah. It too is remarkable because Jesus is so clearly identified for the first Christian community as the fulfilment of the hopes of Israel. Although Jews expected a messiah, no one expected that the Messiah would be God incarnate (in the flesh). This leads to the third title, 'Only Begotten Son', and the one related to it, 'Son of the Father'. Jesus, the historical person with whom the disciples ate and drank both before and after his death and resurrection, is the unique Son who existed with the Father and Holy

Spirit from the beginning. The fourth title reinforces the divine identity of Jesus by simply calling him Lord God, the same expression used in the second stanza for the Father.

'Lamb of God' is a title applied to Jesus in the Scriptures. He is referred by John the Baptist as the lamb of God and, in the Gospel of John, Jesus is represented as the Pascha (Passover) Lamb, who gives up his life. In the Liturgy of the Eucharist, the consecrated bread and wine will simply be called the Lamb of God. Jesus is the Lamb of God who takes away the sins of the world and through whom the Father's mercy comes down upon us and brings forgiveness. As both victim and priest, Christ can intercede for us and is described as seated at the right hand of God. This latter expression also meaning that Jesus is exalted into the Divine Presence.

The final stanza is again addressed to Jesus. He is addressed by four titles. Each of the statements is an affirmation of the faith of the Church in him. Jesus alone is the 'Holy One', the 'Lord', the 'Most High' and the 'Christ'. The first three of these terms come from the Jewish tradition of Jesus and the first Christian communities and are all titles applied to God the Father. Jesus is all of these things 'with the Holy Spirit and the glory of God the Father'. That is, whatever can be said about the Son, can be said about the Father, and the Holy Spirit, while maintaining distinction in the communion of the Holy Trinity.

We conclude with an 'Amen' (a Hebrew word) to affirm our assent to all of these truths which we have prayed. We make these statements our own. We may not do so with a fully formed theological comprehension of each of the statements and titles but we can do so knowing that this is the faith of the Church and the faith that we profess together.

This hymn, the Gloria, is a very ancient one. It was composed in the early centuries of the life of the Church. The composition draws on affirmations of faith that come to us from the first generations of Christians that find expression in Scripture. The words of the first witnesses to Jesus' words, deeds, his dying and his rising, become our words because they are handed onto us from generation to generation for over two thousand years.

The singing of this hymn comes immediately before we pray the collect (opening prayer) and listen to the Word of God proclaimed in the readings. It is as if the hymn prepares us for the presence of Christ whose voice will be heard in the Scriptures proclaimed. It is a hymn worth pondering throughout the week. Take some time to savour each line of the hymn and repeat it slowly a number of times. Let the words sink in. Ponder how profound each statement is about Jesus and the presence of God among us. The angels announce this presence as good tidings for all the world. How do we bring these good tidings to others so that they can know the peace of Christ?

20

Easter, every Sunday

Every now and then, I find myself in a parish – when Mass is about to commence – where there is an announcement from a commentator. The usual welcome to visitors is made, a reminder to turn off mobile phones is given and sometimes other messages are shared. Sometimes, there is included a kind of short summary of the readings for today, sometimes accompanied by the words, 'the theme for our Mass today is...' The 'theme' proposed is either a common thread found in the readings or some special occasion like social justice Sunday. There may be a common theme in the readings (and should be with the first reading and the Gospel) or a special focus of a day such as social justice Sunday, but this is not actually *the* theme of the Mass.

The Mass has the same theme every Sunday and in fact every time it is celebrated. The Mass is a participation in the death and resurrection of Jesus. The central feast and the highest point of the liturgical calendar is Holy Saturday Paschal Vigil. Easter (Pascha) is the point around which the entire year of the Catholic and Orthodox calendars is constructed. Every Sunday is a small-scale celebration of the central Easter/paschal mystery. We have Easter every week.

As you may know, Jesus, the apostles and all of the first followers of Jesus were Jews. For a number of centuries, there remained Jewish and gentile (non-Jewish) members of the Christian community. For Jews, Shabbat (Sabbath), which commences at sunset on Friday and ends at sunset on Saturday, is the day of rest. Observant Jews will gather for a Shabbat meal on Friday evening and enjoy a complete day of rest from all work and many will attend synagogue to pray with others. Shabbat is the seventh and last day of the week.

The first day of the week is the day named after the Sun, Sunday, in the Greek and Roman calendars which we have inherited. It was on the first day of the week, early in the morning, that the women went to the tomb and found it empty. It was on Sunday that Peter and the other Apostles also came to learn of the resurrection. It is on Sunday that Jesus appeared to the women in the garden and later to other disciples. Sunday took on special significance for the first Christian communities, even though most would have observed Shabbat.

The first day of the week became so significant to Christians because it was the day on which Jesus rose from the dead; even in Paul's letters, written in the first decades after Jesus' death and resurrection, he will refer to it as 'the Lord's Day'. We know from the Scriptures and documents written in the first century of the Christian era that women and men would gather on the first day of the week to recall the teaching of the apostles and to share in the sacred meal of bread and wine, using the words we use today: 'Take and eat, this is my body; take and drink, this is my blood, the blood of a new and everlasting covenant'.

These first communities understood that commemorating Jesus' death and resurrection until he comes again was a participation with him in the sacrifice which he had made once and for all. Every time they gathered; they were aware that they were participating in the central mystery of Easter/Pascha. Like the women on that first Easter, they gathered before dawn on Sunday for the practical reason that the first day of the week was a work day in the ancient world. Out of necessity they had to gather before work commenced but out of devotion, they gathered to participate in the presence of Jesus in this privileged moment.

Perhaps as fewer Jews and more gentiles became members of the Christian community, the Shabbat as a sacred day became less significant for communities. In the course of centuries, Christians would stop recognising Sabbath as the holy day and adopt the first day of the week, Sunday, as their holy day.

During the week, there is a mini-Easter theme embedded in the Catholic calendar. The Liturgy of the Hours (Divine Office) on Fridays has a number of references to the death of Christ in an echo of Good Friday. The Liturgy of the Hours is the Prayer of the Church that clergy and religious pray and all lay people can also pray. The other aspect of our calendar is penance on Fridays.

Friday is a day of penance for Catholics because it is a preparation for Sunday and a reminder of Good Friday. Previously, the penance was imposed. That was why we did not eat meat on Fridays. During the 1970s, most bishops changed the way we do Friday penance by asking us to decide either to abstain from meat, spend additional time in prayer, do some good works, go to Mass or choose some other penance to help us prepare for Sunday. The purpose of the penance is not the thing we refrain from or take up, but to focus our hearts and minds on the central mystery of the death and resurrection which we are to celebrate on Sunday.

Every Mass has the theme of the death and resurrection of Jesus. Perhaps you can think about how you will prepare yourself and your family on Friday. What penance can you do or re-introduce to your family practice? Meatless Fridays or seeking out additional good works to do, and even finding a period to sit in silence may be ways in which you can mark out Friday as a day of preparation are all possibilities. Perhaps every Friday you could spend a little time in prayer before a cross or crucifix to meditate on that first Good Friday. In this way, you have a little reminder of the rhythm of Holy Week and you can turn your heart and mind toward the Paschal Mystery. Every Sunday is a little celebration of Easter.

21

Moving parts – opening prayer

I take a regular walk down to a small island that is now connected by a park to the shore and which has good views along a wide stretch of the harbour. I don't think the view is ever the same on any day I have made this walk. The colour of the water varies so much with changes in the sky, the wind some days creates small waves with little white peaks and on other days the water is smooth like glass. There are also variations in the kinds of sea craft I see go by the island. Some days, there are large oil tankers, other days a ferry passes by, a sleek yacht or some other pleasure craft. Each journey to the island is, in some respects, unique and unrepeatable.

When I go to Mass, it is the same kind of unique and unrepeatable experience. Mass is not the same every week. It is not the same because a number of elements of it change each week that provide its unique character. Just as different sea craft appear on the harbour, there are moving parts in the Mass that make an appearance at different times. One of these moving parts is the collect or what some refer to as the opening prayer.

The collect is prayed after the Gloria, when it is sung, or after the penitential act on days when the Gloria is not included in the Mass. (The Gloria is not included in Mass during Lent.) Like almost all of the prayers of the Mass, this is one that we are all praying, not just the one who is presiding at Mass. We know that it is all of us praying because it is introduced with the words, 'Let us pray'. The plural means that even though the presider is speaking the words, he is doing so in the name of the whole church that is assembled here.

It is helpful when there is a short pause before the presider begins to speak the words in our name. The 'let us pray' verse is used frequently in the liturgy and celebration of the sacraments. Its purpose is twofold; first to gain our attention and secondly to help us prepare our ears, hearts and minds to pray the text by joining ourselves with the prayer. When we become attentive, we can more fully join ourselves to the prayer and recall that Christ is praying through, with and in his body the Church.

Each Mass has its own collect. The prayer is addressed to God through Christ and concludes with an invocation of the Holy Trinity. We add our assent to the prayer by responding with 'Amen'. Amen is a Hebrew word and means something like yes or I agree, and similar kinds of sentiments. The use of our amen signifies our joining with the content of this prayer.

The collect highlights some aspect of the mysteries of our faith that we ponder in this particular celebration of the Mass. Throughout the course of the year, all of the central doctrines and beliefs of the Church are celebrated and recalled in Mass as we ponder more deeply the meaning of Christ's life, death and resurrection. If you attend Mass every Sunday, you would learn almost everything there is to know about the Catholic faith. The Mass can help teach and form us in our Catholic faith.

The collects for each Mass are printed in a daily Mass book. It may help you become more attentive to the collect if you read the text before coming to Mass and ponder the meaning of it. Let's look at two examples of collects to illustrate what I mean about highlighting some mystery. The first one is from Wednesday of the second week of Easter and the second from the nineteenth Sunday in Ordinary Time.

Wednesday, Week 2, Easter	*19th Sunday Ordinary Time*
As we recall year by year the mysteries by which, through the restoration of its original dignity, human nature has received the hope of rising again, we earnestly beseech your mercy, Lord, that what we celebrate in faith we may possess in unending love.	Almighty ever living God, whom, taught by the Holy Spirit, we dare to call our Father, bring, we pray, to perfection in our hearts the spirit of adoption as your sons and daughters, that we may merit to enter into the inheritance which you have promised.

From the Easter collect, we see that because of the mystery of Christ's death and resurrection and our baptism into that mystery, the original dignity human beings possessed from creation has been restored. What was destroyed by the first Adam is restored in the Second Adam (Jesus). We also learn that we have the hope of resurrection. The mysteries we celebrate in faith are not simply intellectual ideas or doctrines to know but are something we are to hold onto with unending love. We are to fall in love with the mystery of our restoration, our hope in the resurrection and in Jesus who makes these things possible.

In the Ordinary Time collect, we ponder different mysteries. We recall that Jesus said that the Holy Spirit would remain with us and be our teacher. Even though Jesus is not physically present as our teacher, we continue as his disciples to learn and grow in our faith if we are open to the Spirit teaching us. We have been taught to address God as our Father. We are asking that God will perfect in our hearts the spirit of adoption. The heart is the ancient way of saying the centre of our being, the core of who we are, our essential self. At that level we want to know what it really means to be a son and daughter of God. Because we are sons and daughters, we can receive an inheritance. A remarkable change has come about because we have been baptised into Christ. We can inherit a place in the eternal life.

There is so much to meditate upon and ponder in these simple few lines of prayer that we call the collect. Meditating on these prayers could enrich our praying of them and thereby enrich our experience of the Mass.

22

Times and seasons

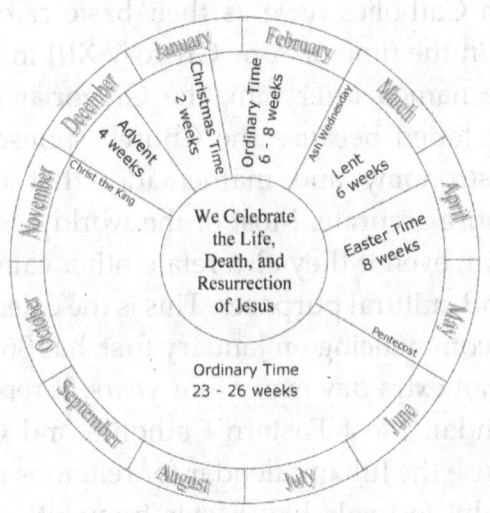

We are all familiar with the four seasons of the year – Summer, Winter, Spring and Autumn. In Australia, these four are reversed in time from the calendar year they hold in their European setting. We have a hot and sweltering Christmas Day and they have a cold, dark and in some places snowy Christmas Day. The Australian Aboriginal people have different ways of dividing up the seasons and these ways correspond much more closely to the true climatic changes that occur during the year in their region. They vary from country to country. In Ngurrungurrudjba country (Northern Australia in Kakadu National Park), six seasons are recognised:

Kudjewk, Bangkerreng, Yekke, Wurrkeng, Kurrung, and Kunumeleng. Around the world, there are many cultures that mark out calendars and seasons in different ways. The Catholic Church has its ways of marking out times and seasons too.

Western Catholics have as their basic calendar one developed in the time of Pope Gregory XIII in 1582. The calendar is named after him, the Gregorian calendar. It was developed because the Church sponsored new work in astronomy and mathematics that made the calendar more accurate. Most of the world has adopted this calendar, even if they also retain other calendars for religious and cultural purposes. This is the calendar with 12 months commencing on January first, has 365 and 1/4 days, with an extra day every four years. It replaced the Julian calendar. Most Eastern Catholics and Orthodox Christians use the Julian calendar for religious purposes, which is why festivals like Easter frequently occur on different dates for Western and Eastern Catholics.

The Latin Catholic calendar or liturgical year is divided into four seasons and one of these four is itself divided into two parts. The liturgical year commences with the first Sunday of Advent. This season occurs over four Sundays and the last week ends with the Nativity (Christmas Day). During Advent, the vestments are purple, sometimes in a lighter shade than Lent vestments. It is a penitential season in which we prepare ourselves for the mystery of the incarnation and Christ's return. It is not as deeply penitential as Lent and that is why the Eastern Churches call it lesser Lent. Each

Sunday, the readings have a character of expectation: the expectation of Israel that the Messiah/Christ will come, the expectation that his birth will come soon, the expectation that he will come again. Advent looks to the past and to the future.

Christmas commences on 25 December which is the Nativity (Birth). It is not Jesus' birthday but a festival that celebrates his birth. This season lasts several weeks and concludes with the celebration of the Baptism of Jesus, which is around mid-January. Within this season, there are a number of festivals. The 'Twelve Days' of Christmas are from Nativity to Epiphany. Epiphany (6/7 January) is a festival in which three things are celebrated: the birth of Jesus, the arrival of the Magi from the East, and the baptism of Jesus. It is from the revelation or epiphany to the nations – symbolised in the arrival of the Magi – that the festival takes its name. For many centuries, this was 'Christmas Day' and remains so for Eastern Catholics and it is the gift-giving day of Christmas in many Western Catholic cultures. Even though the baptism of Jesus is celebrated in the liturgy of Epiphany, it still has its own day, the Baptism of the Lord, which is sometimes called Theophany, because the divine identity of Jesus is revealed. White is the colour of the vestments for this season of Christmas. White is associated with joy.

The first part of the season of Ordinary Time commences after the Baptism of the Lord. The vestments are green which is a traditional symbol of hope. During this time, we begin a semi-continuous reading of the Gospel of Matthew (Year A), Mark (Year B) and Luke (Year C).

Semi-continuous because we follow the Gospel from beginning to end with a few passages either skipped over and others read at a more appropriate time. For example, the texts about Jesus' death and resurrection come at the end of all the Gospels but we read them in the first third of the year, at Easter. During Ordinary time, we are once again disciples, following Jesus on the way from Galilee in northern Israel to Jerusalem in the South and along the way we are taught by him and hopefully grow in our understanding.

We don't get very far into the first part of Ordinary Time (about 6 weeks) before we stop for the season of Lent. Lent commences on Ash Wednesday and will continue for six weeks until we reach Easter. It is a season for fasting, penance and good works to help us focus more clearly on our conversion to the Lord and his teachings. The colour of vestments is purple. We break off our semi-continuous reading of the Gospel and select texts which have a deeper focus on the call to repent and which signal the salvation that is to come through the Easter/Paschal mysteries. We don't sing the Gloria or alleluia during this time because they are joyful hymns. We don't have any other music except when the congregation has to sing; there are no musical interludes or playing of incidental music. We only have music to sing the parts of the Mass and hymns.

The last days of Lent take us to the three holiest days of the Catholic liturgical calendar – Holy Thursday of the Lord's Supper, Good Friday of the Lord's Passion and Holy Saturday Night Paschal Vigil. The Paschal Vigil is the night of nights, the feast of feasts, and represents the pinnacle of the liturgical year. This is the Christian Passover and occurs at the same time as Jewish Passover. Its name comes to us from the Hebrew Pesach (Passover), into Greek *Pascha* and then Latin *Paschal*. When Christian missionaries were taking the Gospel to Germanic and Anglo-Saxon cultures in the early Middle Ages, they encountered a festival celebrated by them during the Spring equinox (when Pascha occurs) which was about new life and light and was devoted to a goddess of Spring *Eostre*, (Easter). The missionaries said we know the true source of life and light and at this time we celebrate his overcoming death. They started to call the Paschal festival, Easter.

Pascha/Easter Vigil occurs on a full moon on the Saturday evening closest to the Spring equinox (in the Northern hemisphere) which is why, as a Lunar festival, it can move around from year to year within a range from March to late April. And because this is the central festival of the Church's year, that means that all the other dates – like commencement of Lent and Advent – also vary. The Paschal or Easter season continues for fifty days in which we focus on the resurrection of Christ and the growth of the first Christian communities. Paschal time concludes with the festival of Pentecost, which is another feast with Jewish origins. Christian Pentecost celebrates the coming of the Holy Spirit and it is sometimes called the birthday of the Church.

Pascha/Easter Vigil occurs on a full moon on the Saturday evening closest to the Spring equinox (in the

Northern hemisphere) which is why, as a Lunar festival, it can move around from year to year within a range from March to late April. And because this is the central festival of the Church's year, that means that all the other dates – like commencement of Lent and Advent – also vary. The Paschal or Easter season continues for fifty days in which we focus on the resurrection of Christ and the growth of the first Christian communities. Paschal time concludes with the festival of Pentecost, which is another feast with Jewish origins. Christian Pentecost celebrates the coming of the Holy Spirit and it is sometimes called the birthday of the Church.

After Pentecost, we return to a longer session (about 25 weeks), of the season of Ordinary Time and pick up the Gospel we were reading and continue on again. Once again, the colour of vestments is green. Some Sundays in Ordinary Time are interrupted by solemnities that concern a particular mystery of faith, the Lord, and his life that is to be celebrated. Some of these include Body and Blood of Christ (*Corpus Christi*) and Trinity Sunday. The last Sunday of Ordinary Time is the Feast of Christ the King. The following Sunday will be the First Sunday of Advent, and the liturgical year commences again. It is quite acceptable to make new year's resolutions on this Sunday and line up your resolutions with the liturgical year and the life, death and resurrection of the Lord. Who know, perhaps by making this link you may actually keep them beyond the end of January!

If your home has a Catholic calendar, like the one created by the Columban Missionary Society, you will always have a reminder of the feasts, solemnities and seasons of the year. It would be good to have something like this in the home to remind you that – just like the traditional owners of country in Australia – there are other ways of marking off days and seasons that give a different meaning to the simple march of secular events during the year. There is a sacred time and sacred seasons that weave their way through our lives each year.

23

Two tables

When we look toward the front of a Catholic Church, two pieces of furniture are very prominent. There is a large table called an Altar in the centre of the space and to the left of it is another table called an Ambo, from which the Scripture portions are proclaimed and the minister will preach. These are the two tables from which we are nourished each week. The Table of the Word and the Table of the Eucharist form a unity and are the two halves of the one meal.

Perhaps we do not associate hearing the Word of God proclaimed with nourishment, in the more obvious way in which bread and wine are like food. In our culture, we do have some references to words as food. When someone makes a claim that is later to be found false, we sometimes say; 'He had to eat his words'. The Prophet Jeremiah says of God's word, 'When your word came [to my mouth] I devoured it.' Jesus says, 'A person does not live on bread alone but on every word that comes from the mouth of God' (Matthew 4:4).

When we come to hear the Word of God proclaimed, we need to imagine ourselves sitting at a table and food – which has been lovingly prepared – is served to us. We need to cultivate an attentive disposition so that our ears and hearts are ready to receive every morsel of this 'food' and we savour it. Some of the saints of long ago would say: be attentive to the Word so that not even a crumb should fall from the table. In the liturgy of the Eastern Catholic Churches, the deacon will chant; 'Wisdom! Be attentive!' before the Scriptures are proclaimed. He tells the congregation to be ready to receive the portion that is to be served.

Sometimes, people tell me that it is hard to be attentive to the Word, that their attention drifts off. I remember a parishioner saying to me, 'I often find that when you say in the homily, as we heard from so and so in our readings today. I have to pick up the bulletin and see who did we hear from today? It has already gone out of my mind'. He was a man in his thirties. He loved to go to the movies and would often recount movies he would recommend that I see. I wondered how was it possible that he could sit through a feature length movie with an intricate plot and was not able to be equally attentive to a few paragraphs from Scripture that had been proclaimed just a minute ago.

I don't know how to train yourself to be more attentive to the Scriptures proclaimed. Perhaps, if you are like the parishioner above, you might pray at the start of Mass, while focusing on the Ambo, 'open my ears to hear your word and open my heart to savour your word'. There is a big difference between hearing and listening. Anyone who has raised teenagers will know that they can often hear what you are saying and the requests to complete tasks that you may make, but when you return from work, the tasks remain to be done. We need to be attentive with our ears to hear the words but we must learn to listen with the ear of the heart to savour the words as St Benedict advises.

The table of the Eucharist is the altar. It is from here that we receive the bread and wine that has become the body and blood of Christ. Because bread and wine are food, we understand the concept of nourishment more concretely. However, it is important to recognise that the two tables are linked and it is helpful to think of them as 'first' and 'second' course of a single meal. We need to let the flavour of the first course mingle with those of the second. In many cultures where there is a sequence of courses for a meal, the flavours, textures and sometimes colour of the foods, are chosen such that each course complements the other and creates one complete meal. Courses are not randomly assembled.

The portions of Scripture served in first course need to be consumed with and joined to the portions served in the Eucharist. The Liturgy of Eucharist does not consist only of the rite of reception of Holy Communion. The prayer over the gifts, the preface and the Eucharistic payers, each contribute to the unique flavour of the Eucharist being celebrated today. It is not only the taste of the bread and wine in our mouth that we consume but these prayers also. We need to be attentive to these words and prayers and gestures because they help as savour the food that is the Eucharist.

Bread is not just bread and wine is not just wine. Anyone who has ventured into a good bakery will know that there are many different styles of bread with their own textures and flavours. The textures and flavours of good bread can enhance a meal for those who love bread. A good baguette or pane di casa from a fine bakery is quite a different experience of bread compared to a loaf of sliced white from the supermarket. A red wine that costs $7 from a discount liquor barn is likely to taste quite different compared to a $60 bottle of red wine from a fine wine merchant.

The bread and wine on offer at Mass is of the high-quality end even though it appears as simple bread and wine. In fact, the bread hardly appears like bread, when it is in the form of a wafer. What the food of the Eucharist has in common with the high-quality bread and wine is the better-quality ingredients and the care taken in its preparation. The ingredient is the Lord himself, so we understand that it cannot be surpassed. In my analogy with quality bread and wine, the careful preparation that enhances the flavour are the words and gestures that surround the preparation of it each week. Both the tables of the Word and Eucharist are equally important to our nourishment and provide us food for the journey of discipleship. We need to cultivate a discerning palette to able to savour the food we receive from each table. What is it that you can do to train yourself to be attentive so that you can be more completely nourished by this food?

24

Pairing the Word

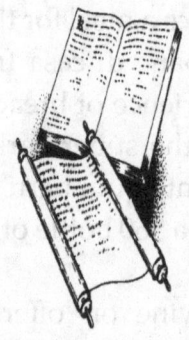

The readings as Mass are chosen with a plan in mind. On Sundays and solemnities, there are three readings; a first reading (normally from the First Testament), a psalm follows, then there is a second reading, normally from one of the letters or other books in the Second Testament and finally a Gospel reading. On week days, there are two readings and a psalm. Knowing how they are chosen and how they relate to each other can assist you in listening to them and gaining some insights from them.

Throughout the course of a year, quite a variety of Scripture texts will be read at Sunday Mass. Over the course of a single Liturgical Year, at least one passage from every book in the Bible will be read at Mass. Sometimes these are very short readings and sometimes they may be longer.

Three Scriptures texts are chosen with a thematic relationship in mind; First Reading, Psalm and Gospel. In selecting the readings which are to be gathered in the Lectionary for Sunday Mass there is a three-year cycle based around the Gospels of Matthew (Year A), Mark (Year B) and Luke (Year C). These three are called the synoptic gospels because when examined together it is clear that they have the same narrative structure of a journey of Jesus from Galilee in the north of Israel to Judea in the South. John does not have this same narrative structure and is used from time to time but does not have a year of its own.

The second reading at Mass has its own cycle and may have no relationship to the Gospel throughout Ordinary Time. During other seasons, the Second Reading is more closely related. Most of the time, it is a semi-continuous reading from one of the Second Testament letters.

Gospel readings are selected first and the First Reading and psalm are chosen to match with the theme found in the portion of the Gospel to be read that day. The advantage the synoptic Gospels have is that their narrative structure makes it easy to pick up one passage each week and continue the narrative. The Gospels are read in a semi-continuous fashion. That is, we commence at the first chapter and move toward the last, except, of course, that the last chapters, that deal with the death and resurrection of Jesus, are read at Easter. Not every passage of the Gospel will be read and a few sections are skipped without departing too much from the basic journey narrative.

A suitable text is chosen from another book of the Bible for the First Reading. This portion of Scripture is chosen because it has a thematic relationship to the Gospel portion which is to be read on that day. Sometimes, the text itself is alluded to or is directly quoted in the Gospel reading. For most of the year, the First Reading will be chosen from one of the books of the First Testament. During Easter, the First Reading mostly comes from the Acts of the Apostles. Listen closely to the First Reading and you will get a hint of themes and ideas that are to come in the Gospel. With the First Reading, sometimes even in a single chapter, only select verses are read in the Scripture portion heard at Mass. For example, there may be a reading from the Prophet Isaiah chapter 42 but only verses one to four and seven and eight. Sometime, the verses skipped over contain material that is not central to the theme around which the selection of the text has been made.

The Responsorial Psalm is chosen to match the same themes and ideas present in the Gospel. Some psalms are very long and normally only a few stanzas of the psalm will be sung. Psalms are songs and where possible they should be sung by a cantor singing the verses and the people singing the response. Frequently, the response carries with it the theme that links to the Gospel reading. Other words and phrases in the psalm will also have connections with the Gospel. Listening carefully as the cantor and people sing allows us to ponder the central themes of Scripture that are unfolding as we read the Bible in this Mass today.

As we noted in earlier sections, this is not the theme of the Mass, just the theme of the readings. Throughout the course of the year, we follow the same journey that the first disciples of Jesus walked with him. Like them, we are learning along the way. You will notice, if you are attentive, that the disciples, even the closet collaborators of Jesus, the Apostles, frequently prove to be hard to instruct and sometimes they make significant mistakes. They were real people, like us in so many ways. They may have had the privilege of speaking with, sharing meals with and just being in the presence of Jesus, but that privilege at that time did not confer on them some special advantage in understanding or of being more faithful than us.

So much of their deep understanding of Jesus' words, deed and his presence came to them as the Holy Spirit became their teacher after Easter. As we know, the Apostles will become the foundation stones on which the Church is built and they will become the chief witnesses and guarantee of faith. That is why we call authentic faith and doctrine the Apostolic faith.

We may live in the time after Easter – and the Holy Spirit is our teacher – but sometimes I think we live the experience of the disciples making that first journey with Jesus. It is as if we are hearing some of this for the first time and we are still making the mistakes of misunderstanding and lack of clear witness that the disciples had before Easter. That is OK. That is not a problem. If we are willing to continue the walk with him and with our companions on the journey, we can open our ears to hear and our hearts to listen and grow in understanding. There are times too, when our faith is strong and we live a life which clearly witnesses to the Gospel. There are times when we live the faith with fervour, devotion and at cost to ourselves in a variety of ways.

In hearing the Scripture portions, we need to remind ourselves that we are the people who live both in the time before Easter and the time after. Not that we deny the reality of Christ Risen. The living between the two times is more about living with what has been accomplished and living what is yet to come in our lives. Disciples are always learners. Disciples are saints and sinners too, but all wait upon the Holy Spirit as our teacher.

25

A cycle within a cycle

I remember some of my nieces and nephews when they were very young watching Sesame Street on T.V. There was a song which accompanied an activity to learn shapes. There may be three circles and a square and the song would go, 'One of these things is not like the other, one of these things just doesn't belong. Can you tell me which one is not like the others before I finish my song?' This song applies to the readings at Mass too. When we place the first reading, psalm, second reading and Gospel beside each other, we can see which one is not like the others. It is the second reading.

When we reflected on the readings in the last section, we learned that the first reading and psalm are both related to the central theme of the Gospel for that day. The second reading, for most of the year (Ordinary Time), has its own cycle and is not chosen because it relates to the Gospel, as are the other readings. Outside of Ordinary Time, the second reading is more frequently related to the Gospel.

It is really helpful to know that this one is not like the others because sometimes what the second reading is about is so far removed from the theme and tone of the other readings that it can almost be jarring. Sometimes, it sounds like the second reading interrupts the flow of the others and is referring to ideas and teachings that are hard to align with the Gospel for the day. One person said to me at an adult faith formation session that the second reading always seemed so random to her that she wondered why we had it.

You may recall that when I mentioned how readings are selected, one of the principles is that, over the course of a year, and taking into account Sunday and Week Day Masses, that we will hear a passage, however small from every book in the Bible. This alerts us to the fact that the Bible, which means book in Greek (Byblos), and which looks very much like a book is in fact is a library of books. Books in libraries are not stacked randomly – there is a classification system.

Catholic and Orthodox Christians have more books in their Bible than Protestants because they use the Greek (Septuagint) version of the First Testament and Protestants do not. The Septuagint is the version which the first Christians used and it is the version mostly quoted in the Second Testament. Christians and Jews classify the books of the First Testament in different ways. The First Testament for Catholics is classified into the following group: The Pentateuch (First five books), Historical books, Wisdom Books, Prophets (Major and Minor).

All Christians have the same number of books and the same order or books in the Second Testament. The books are classified; Gospels, Acts of the Apostles (which is the Gospel of Luke part two), Letters of Paul, Letters to All Christians and Revelation (also called Book of Apocalypse). The second reading is chosen from among all the books other than the Gospels. For most of Ordinary Time, the second reading will come from the letters. At other times, such as the fifty days of Easter, the second reading mostly comes from Acts of the Apostles, which recount the post-resurrection experience of the Church.

During ordinary time, we have a semi-continuous reading from the letters of the Second Testament. The letters have their own system of organisation. For example, the letters of Paul are not arranged in the order in which he wrote them but in order from longest letter to shortest. Each letter also has a particular audience and sometimes a particular question or problem in the Christian community with which it is primarily concerned. When you hear the title 'A letter of St Paul to the Romans', this means the Church in the city of Rome, a community that existed before Paul's letter which comes from the mid-fifties AD. It helps if you can picture each of these as communities of Christians hearing Paul's letters read when they gathered for worship. Most of the letters, especially those of Paul, pre-date the Gospels.

Because of the varied audiences, varied questions and problems, and the fact that they are not chronological, we are reading selections from them which may, for a few weeks, bear some common thematic elements and then the next week a completely new topic is introduced. There is not the same sustained narrative that we find in the Gospel readings. The questions and problems which are being addressed in the letters have no connection with questions, problems or audience being addressed in the Gospel portion of the day. So, the woman in the adult faith formation session was fairly accurate in her description – they do indeed seem random, but they are not. They are just on a cycle of readings which is within a bigger cycle of the other readings.

I have sometimes heard preachers who have bravely attempted always to include the Second Reading in a homily but they often stretch the text too far to squeeze it into the theme of the Gospel for the day. Sometimes, these homilies end up just been a commentary on all the readings for the day. If a preacher really wants to get the most out of the Second Reading to enrich the congregation, he should focus just on that text and elaborate from there and not try to artificially fit all readings together when they we not designed to be together.

To the second part of the woman's comment – about why do we have this reading? – there are several answers. First, it is because they are sacred Scripture and Christ speaks to us through this word proclaimed. Second, because there are rich themes on which we can meditate and enrich our faith that are not articulated in this same way in other books of the Second Testament. Third, because often the readings touch on questions

A cycle within a cycle

and problems which we still experience within the Christian community today. It is sometimes amazing to discover how their problems and challenges seem so contemporary with ours.

When we know the Second Reading has its own cycle within the cycle of the other readings, we are better prepared when they just don't fit together. We will be less distracted by this apparent clash. The letters are a rich source for nurturing Christian faith and they should be read and meditated upon so as to deepen that faith.

26

Welcoming the Gospel

Within the Liturgy of the Word at Mass, it is obvious that the Gospel reading is treated differently to the other readings from the Bible. The proclamation of the Gospel is a high point of the Liturgy of the Word. Jesus comes to us in the word of the Gospel in a way that is distinct from the other readings.

All the readings for Mass are extracted from the Bible and re-produced in a book of readings called the Lectionary. The Gospel readings for the day are also included in the lectionary but they can be proclaimed from a special book of Gospels called an Evangeliary. Gospel comes to us through Germanic languages as a translation of the phrase 'good news'. In Koine Greek, a message of good tidings or news is *euangelion* (eu-ang-gel-ion) or evangelion from which we get our words evangelise, evangelical and similar. The Gospel of Mark begins with the sentence, 'A beginning of the good news (*euangelion*) of Jesus Christ...' and this good news or gospel became the generic name for the group of books that primarily recount Jesus' words and deeds and his death and resurrection; the Gospels.

If a Book of Gospels is to be used at Mass, there are two different ways in which it enters the Church at Mass. If there is no deacon, the Book of Gospels is simply placed on the altar before Mass, in the spot where the chalice and patten will later be placed. If there is a deacon, he brings in the book during the entry procession, holding it slightly elevated, and places it on the altar as above. The Book of Gospels is closely identified with deacons who were chosen to proclaim the Gospel and they receive the Evangeliary at their ordination as the primary symbol of their ministry. The Lectionary is not normally processed into the Church. It is simply placed on the Ambo before Mass.

When it is time to proclaim the Gospel, there are a number of rituals which signify that this reading has a special place in the life of the Church. The first ritual element is the singing of a verse before the Gospel. Except during Lent, alleluia is sung during the Gospel verse. It can be sung as long as it takes for the Book of Gospels to go from the altar to Ambo. All stand to greet the Gospel with this verse.

If incense is to be used (and it should be at least at every Sunday Mass in my view), the presbyter or bishop places some grains of incense onto the hot charcoal and blesses it. If there is a deacon, he seeks a blessing from the one who is presiding. He asks; 'Father, give me your blessing'. The presider makes the sign of the cross over him while praying; 'May the Lord be on your lips and in your heart that you may proclaim his holy Gospel worthily and well'. When a presbyter is alone for Mass, he says the same prayer in preparation for the proclamation of the Gospel but changes 'your' to 'my' and 'you' to 'I'. A deacon proceeds to pick up the Book of Gospels and processes to the Ambo following the incense and candle bearers. If there is no Book of Gospels, after the blessing, he heads directly to the Ambo and reads from the Lectionary.

Once the deacon has placed the Book of Gospels on the Ambo, he greets the people. With hands joined, a deacon, presbyter or bishop, will use the same greeting before the Gospel; 'The Lord be with you'. The people respond, 'And with your spirit'. In this way, they acknowledge that the Lord Jesus is standing in our midst and is about to address us through the Gospel. He will announce, 'A reading from the Holy Gospel according to N'. As he says these words, he will trace a cross on the Gospel portion to be proclaimed and sign his forehead, lips and heart. The congregation will do them same. In response to the announcement, 'A reading from...' the people respond, 'Glory to you, O Lord'. We are acknowledging that we are not so much hearing Matthew, Mark of Luke but the voice of the Lord.

As we make the triple sign of the cross on forehead, lips and heart, perhaps we can pray, 'May your word be in my thoughts, in my words and in my heart'. This is a gesture and prayer that we can make every time that we open the Bible to read a text. The prayer can help us become disposed toward pondering and savouring God's word and allowing this word to transform us into what we receive.

If incense is to be used, the deacon or presbyter incenses the Book with three double swings, centre, left and then right. He hands the thurible to the server or acolyte who stands behind him and swings it during the proclamation of the Gospel. Altar servers who accompanied the procession with candles stand on either side of the Ambo. The Gospel may be read or chanted, without musical accompaniment. At the conclusion of the reading, the deacon or presbyter does not lift the book but looks at the people and says or chants, 'The Gospel of the Lord'. The people respond, 'Praise to you Lord Jesus Christ'. The deacon or presbyter may bend to the book or lift it to his lips and kisses the book, saying quietly, 'Through the words of the Gospel may our sins be wiped away'. If a bishop presides at Mass. the deacon or presbyter takes the Book of Gospels to the bishop to venerate with a kiss and he may take the book, close it and bless the congregation by making the sign of the cross with it, as the people trace the sign on their own bodies.

Why do so many rituals surround the proclamation of the Gospel? The reason seems to be that we want to venerate the Gospel because in it we hear Jesus' words and experience his presence in a unique manner. It is as if Jesus himself has come to stand in our midst and speak to us directly. We should allow ourselves to imagine that this is exactly what is happening. When the deacon (or presbyter) stands before, us we are to see not the deacon but Jesus. We are to hear not the voice of the deacon, but Jesus. Perhaps just at that that moment before the reading itself commences, we could pray, 'Jesus, open my ears and heart to hear you'. If we hear God's word and live it out in our lives, then we can become good news, gospel, for others.

27

Receiving the Word

It is not easy to give a good homily. Lots of those who preach know this. It takes time to prepare a good homily. The texts have to be read several times and pondered deeply in prayer. Commentaries need to be studied and some deeper understanding about the text needs to be achieved. The texts need to be connected to the liturgy, the liturgical season and the world in which we live our faith. Effort, energy, time and prayer are necessary ingredients for a good homily. Then it needs to be delivered in way that in comprehensible and with some reasonable oratorial skill.

Lots of people who come to Mass week in and week out also know that preparing a good homily is not easy because surveys of Catholics reveal that they so rarely seem to find preaching that is uplifting and nurtures their spirits. Many surveys among Catholics reveal that they frequently do not experience good homilies; and that they wish that they were better. Benedict XVI said once to a group of presbyters that it was a testament to the resilience of the faith of lay Catholics that they came back to Mass each week in spite of the preaching of the clergy.

Homilies have taken on a lot of importance in the life of most Catholics because it is one of the primary ways in which they are informed about and formed in the Catholic faith. The homily has become a moment of adult catechesis or instruction. Some surveys reveal that Catholics often regard the homily as the highlight and most memorable part of Mass. Of course, I believe that good and even excellent homilies should be the order of the day for every Mass but the reality is that clergy are not always going to deliver this and perhaps, for some, preaching in not their gift. I have met presbyters who are never going to set the world on fire with a homily but, day in day out, they set the world on fire through their deep pastoral engagement, reaching out to the poor and marginalised, strengthening weak parishioners, giving deep words of comfort to a bereaved parishioner and many more acts in which the fire of God's love touches lives. Yes, a good homily is required but it is not the sole measure of what is important in the Mass and the life of the parish.

It may seem counter intuitive but a homily is not primarily about the words of the homilist. The purpose of a homily is to assist the people to receive the Word of God. It is the counterpart to the reception of Holy Communion in the liturgy of the Eucharist. At the end of the homily, we don't want to be thinking about how clever and thoughtful the words of the preacher were or how well he delivered the homily. At the end of the homily, we want to be pondering, savouring and digesting the Word of God we have heard proclaimed. If both the homilist and people keep in mind that the purpose of the homily is to assist us all, homilist included, to receive God's Word and live it out in our lives, perhaps we will hear better homilies but also gain more from them.

I am happy to report that sometimes, certainly not all the time, I have had people come to me after Mass and say, 'I really enjoyed your homily today'. I always ask, what it was that they liked about it. Many times, they have replied with something that moved them or caused them to think more deeply about something and sometimes they even attempt to quote me. What is very humbling is that frequently I actually did not say what they quote back to me or the profound thought that moved them was not what I thought was the point of my homily or perhaps was a minor point I thought I was making along the way. Yet they have been moved and received something from my words. What this experience has revealed to me is, that this is precisely the point of a homily. They are not to receive my word but the Word of God. My homily has been the catalyst which has made that connection possible. They have been moved by the Spirit and not by my words. If the homily has done some good to nurture their spirits, it is all God's work, not mine.

The homily is about assisting the people to receive the Word of God and it is ultimately God's work and not that of the preacher. This does not absolve the preacher from the grave obligation to prepare a good homily each week.

I have two quotes in front of me when I prepare a homily. The first is from the Biblical scholar Walter Burghardt, 'The unprepared homilist is a menace. I do not discount the inspiration of the Holy Spirit but find such inspiration is rarely given to the lazy'. The second is from a book on the new evangelisation by Archbishop Rino Fisichella, 'To give an unprepared homily is to dishonour the Word of God and to force a humiliation on the laity'. I try to take both of these sentiments seriously in preparing my own homilies. Yet I can say that not every homily I have given has hit the mark and allowed people to receive the Word of God as effectively as they should. Let's encourage and support our preachers and given them feedback, in charity, that will allow them to improve. By all means encourage better preaching. You deserve it and have a right to it.

We also need to look to our own disposition in hearing a homily, whether it be a good, bad or indifferent homily. When we sit to listen to the homily, first pray for the homilist that he will proclaim the Gospel worthily and well. Then pray for the gift of attentiveness so that you will be ready to receive God's Word. Listen with the ears and the heart. There should be a few moments of silence after the homily. During this silence turn your attention to the Scriptures proclaimed and the homily just heard. Ask yourself – what is the one thing I need to hear from God's Word today? Sit and ponder on that in your heart and allow yourself to receive God's Word.

28

I set my heart on...

What is it that you have set your heart on? Have you ever had the experience of setting your heart on something or someone? Perhaps, if you are married, you may recall when you set your heart on your beloved. Perhaps you have set your heart on obtaining a particular qualification, or getting a particular job. Perhaps a house that you thought was so ideal for you that you had set your heart on purchasing it. There may be a number of times when you look back over your life that you can recall setting your heart on something or someone.

When we think about heart this way, we obviously do not mean the organ that pumps blood around our body. We understand heart to be a metaphor. We mean something like a complete commitment of will, intellect and emotion. Depending on what or who it is, on which we have set our heart, one of these three may be a more dominant aspect of our longing and commitment. In a sense, we use heart as a metaphor for the whole of myself or a holistic commitment.

This brings me to the Creed. After the homily and the period of silence to reflect on and digest the Word of God, we stand to recite the Creed. In the Roman Rite the Nicene Creed is the normal one for Sunday Mass as this is the one most Christian churches and communities recite. The Apostles Creed may be used in the Easter seasons, because of its close parallel to the Baptism promises. This second creed is only used by Latin or Roman Catholics.

We are literally standing up for our faith when we stand to recite the creed. We are standing up to be counted among those who profess the faith of the Catholic Church. We pray this prayer in the first person singular, 'I'. Although we pray it together, this is one of the few prayers of the Mass which we pray in our own name. If we were baptised as infants then as we grow older, we begin to recite the creed that others recited for us. We make it our own. We need to find ways of making it truly our own and truly a prayer and not just a list or catalogue of Christian doctrines.

Creed comes from the Latin *credo*, I believe. *Credo* has its roots in a Greek word, *kardia* or heart (cardiac arrest or cardiology are derived from Greek too). When we pray the Creed, we are not so much saying 'I believe' in an intellectual sense, we are saying 'I set my heart on...' We are praying about our whole commitment of self to what it is that we pray. Try this at home. Instead of saying I believe say, 'I set my heart on God the father... I set my heart on God the Son, ... I set my heart on the Holy Spirit and I set my heart on the Church...' Read the prayer through slowly and ponder each of the statements on which you have set your heart.

How different the words appear and the commitment seems when we shift our language from 'I believe' to 'I set my heart on'. In our modern use of the word 'believe', we have come to think of it mostly as an intellectual commitment, something associated with our head and minds. We don't immediately associate it with the heart and our total commitment. Yet this is what we are saying. These are the commitments; these are the longings upon which my heart is set and I seek this more than all else. Jesus says, 'For where your treasure is, there your heart will be also' (Matthew 6:21) and, 'Blessed are the pure in heart, for they will see God.' (Matthew 5:8)

The Creed does not tell us everything about Christian faith. It is a summary of some central teachings that define us. We set our heart upon God, who is one and yet three Persons, Father, Son and Holy Spirit. It is upon God, revealed as a Holy Trinity, upon which we have set our hearts. We want to know and love God who has been revealed to us in this way. As a Christian community, we somehow know that setting our heart upon God will lead to our own full flourishing as human beings.

I set my heart on... the whole universe as touched by the presence of God created by the Father, through the Son in the Holy Spirit. I set my heart on the Creator of the universe who came among us, fully human, as one like us in all things (consubstantial) except sin and remained fully God (consubstantial with the Father). I set my heart on... the crucified and risen one who has conquered death and opens the way to resurrection for us. I set my heart upon God the Holy Spirit who breathes life into us and pours out grace abundantly in and through the holy Church, which is Christ's body. I set my heart upon… the completion of all creation, the emergence of the Kingdom in its fulness when Jesus returns and there will be a new heaven and a new earth. I don't just believe these things as an intellectual proposition or an idea; I set my heart on these as those things which fundamentally orient my life and give it direction. This is what I long for, this is what I desire and this is what I would give everything else away to possess - this is the great treasure found in a field, the one treasure upon which I can set my heart (Matthew 13:44).

Next time, before you go to Mass, spend some time in meditation on the Creed. Ponder it as something upon which you have set your heart. Savour the words by reciting before each statement about the Father, Son Holy Spirit and the Church; 'I set my heart upon'. In time, begin to write a personal creed about your deep commitment to faith and life. When you come to Mass, you can more deeply pray from your heart the words of the Creed.

29

Calling to mind the Church and world

Most of us arrive at Mass having something on our minds. It may simply be the struggles we have had getting the children ready and out the door to get to Mass reasonably on time. It may be the aches and pains we seem to feel each morning as we grow older. Sometimes, we have in our mind the stress of unemployment, a recently received diagnosis of a major illness, the sadness of the death of a family member or friend, the joy of a recently announced engagement or birth of a child and so many other hopes, joys, anxieties and sorrows. Just because we are at Mass, we don't switch off from or disconnect from any of this.

Rather than see these kinds of things as distractions from Mass, bring them with you to Mass. Make these your special intentions for the Mass which you are about to celebrate. Hand them over to God, join them with the offering of the Mass. God can hold all of our stresses and strains without breaking, whereas they may break us. God can bless our joys and affirm our spirits, in times of celebration and hope and in times of sorrow. You can truly be yourself before God and open up all aspects of your life to God. What better place to do this than in the Mass, to offer up your joys and hopes and anxieties with the offering of this perfect and unending sacrifice which Christ gave on the Cross.

Everyone who joins you at Mass today – presbyter, deacon and people – also bring what is on their minds with them to Mass. Just as you may be sitting or kneeling before Mass sharing with God your thoughts and prayers, so are they. You are never alone at Mass and never alone in bringing your intentions before God. There is comfort in knowing that each one is sharing their concerns and joys with God just as you are. In a sense, you are weaving a tapestry of prayer intentions together with all who are present. Each one contributing a thread or two to the whole. Or, to take another image, if you imagine each one typing out their intentions, you are each contributing a line to a whole page of text.

The many become one through the offering and receiving of the one bread and the one cup. You are joined together as the Body of Christ, the Church, in this place and in this particular Mass. All who are gathered for Mass in this place with you are joined with the wider communion of the Church and in bonds of communion with all people. After we pray the Creed, we remain standing and offer the Universal Prayer, known also as the Prayers of the Faithful. In these prayers, we join our particular intentions with those of the wider Church and world. A deacon announces the Universal Prayer, and, if there is no deacon, a lay person announces them.

Although parishes frequently use a book of Universal Prayers for this part of the Mass, that is not necessary. It is best if they are composed by the deacon or lay person who is to proclaim them, using a standard responsorial model as may be found in such books. The intentions only need to be short and few in number. Because they are the prayers of the faithful, we all stand and all respond, 'Lord, hear our prayer' or similar responses, so that we make the prayer our own.

Generally, we start with the needs of the Church. Some of these intentions may be for the parish and people and events in the parish. For example, we might pray for those preparing for baptism or those entering into full communion, or for a spirit of prayer during a parish mission. We may then include some intentions connected with the local Church (diocese). Perhaps we might pray for our bishop and deacons and presbyters or we might pray for the success of a youth convention being held in the diocese or for other intentions concerning the life of the local Church. The needs of the universal Church should be included so that we recall that we are part of a bigger communion of Churches. These intentions for the universal Church may include prayers for the Bishop of Rome (the Pope), events like synods and councils and support for missionaries and evangelists.

All Christians share some, though not full, communion with the Catholic Church. It is good to pray for other Christians and even particular Christian communities close to your local Church. We might pray that they will be effective in the ministry of the Gospel, or ask God's blessing on a newly installed pastor and we might pray for the day when we might share full communion with each other.

The last intention is usually for the recently deceased and those whose anniversary of death occurs around this time. In the Book of Maccabees we are urged to pray for the deceased, for forgiveness of their sins. They are a part of us and we pray for one another.

Gaudium et Spes, or the Pastoral Constitution on the Church in the Modern World (Vatican II) says; 'The hopes and joys, the griefs and anxieties of women and men in our day, especially those who are poor and afflicted, are the joys and hopes, the griefs and anxieties of the followers of Christ. In fact, nothing that is genuinely human fails to find an echo in their hearts'. It is for this reason that we include the intentions of men and women in our local area, our nation and world in our prayers. We may include such intentions as bush fires, pandemic and sickness, environmental issues, justice for and reconciliation with Aboriginal and Torres Strait Islander people and other First Nations People around the world, as well as many other issues that touch the lives of people.

We want to call to mind the Church and the world in this particular Mass, in this particular place and to join these intentions with the offering of the Mass for the peace and salvation of all. Before the prayer begins, in that brief moment before they are proclaimed, you might pray; 'Lord, I want to join my intentions with those of the Church and world and offer it all to you'.

30

Presenting ourselves

Normally, the bread and wine to be offered at Mass are brought to the presbyter by some of the congregation. At the same time, the collection of money for the support of the clergy and the works of the Church may be presented as well. The table with the bread and wine to be brought up may be placed in the middle and sometimes the back of smaller churches. The procession of the gifts from the people to the altar, though short and without much ceremony, is a profound procession. For it is not just a movement of the bread and wine but of the whole Church toward the altar.

The gifts come from among us and in a sense represent us. They are placed in our midst to express the fact that the gifts come from this people. In the earliest centuries of the Latin Rite, the bread was baked at home by a parishioner and brought to the gifts table. This is still the custom in some Eastern Catholic and Orthodox

Churches. In ancient times, and still in some cultures today, the presentation of gifts not only includes the bread and wine, but sometimes other gifts of food and gifts for the poor of the community. In most wealthy countries such as our own, the only time we see these additional gifts being present may occur during Lent with the collection for Project Compassion.

Bringing the gifts up from the congregation is a sign of the gathering of the congregation into one communion. The prayer over the gifts in the Syrian and Chaldean Catholic Churches refers to the many grains gathered to form the bread and the many grapes gathered to make the wine. The baptised are those many grains of wheat and the many grapes gathered. We need to be able to see with the eyes of faith that it is ourselves that has been gathered up and harvested and placed upon the altar.

In one of his homilies, St Augustine invites us to look at the bread and wine as it is placed upon the altar as a sign of ourselves. We are like Isaac placed upon the altar of sacrifice. We are joined to Christ in Baptism and have become his Body and it is this body which is placed upon the altar. We are joined intimately to what is to be offered.

Jesus is one like us in our humanity (consubstantial) except he is without sin. He is, in the words of one of the Eucharistic Prayers, a 'spotless Victim, a pure Victim'. Although we are joined to him in baptism and placed upon the altar, it is not an offering of ourselves but a joining of ourselves to his once and for all offering on the Cross that can bring healing and salvation. We only offer Christ in the Eucharist. This distinction may seem small but it is significant. We are not the author or cause of our own salvation. We are not a perfect or pure sacrifice offered upon the altar.

It is worth pondering this for a moment and not letting the offertory procession and the presentation of the gifts pass us by. God is able to accept us – the many grains and the many grapes – with all of our faults and with all of our imperfections. We who are caught up in sin and weakness and who let ourselves and others down, even as we strive to live a Christian life; we are acceptable to God. In fact, we can place our very weakness and our many failed attempts to be the person that we ought to be, a true sign of the love of Christ toward others. We can place all of the good and wonderful things about ourselves on the altar with the bread and wine, as well as all of the parts of which we are not proud and which represent our weakness and failure.

Let's not fall into the trap of thinking I have to be worthy to be placed upon this altar. When we think this way, we are, in fact, making ourselves the author of our own salvation. We imagine that through some effort of our own we can save ourselves or make ourselves perfect. Then, once we are perfect, we think we will be worthy to be placed upon the altar. This attitude reveals a lack of trust in Jesus when he says, 'Come to me all who are heavy burdened and I will give your rest'. Our task is to open ourselves to the working of the grace of Jesus Christ in us when the Spirit is poured out upon us. Grace builds on and transforms our nature. Nature does not transform grace. All is gift. All grace is freely given. We need to open wide our hearts and hands to receive this grace.

When we see the bread and wine placed upon the altar, we can truly pray, 'Lord, I place my life upon this altar. Take all that I am and all that I have. I give all my life to you. Join me to the offering of Christ that I may be lifted up and become that which I am about receive, the Body of Christ'. Hold no part of your life back and in this way all parts of your life may be transformed. Trust in God and allow yourself to be gathered up in the harvest of baptism and Eucharist and one day be gathered into the harvest of the Kingdom of God.

31

Preparation of the Gifts

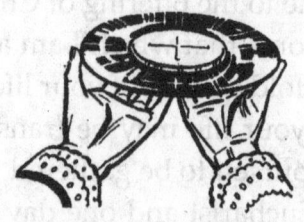

Once the gifts have reached the altar, and an exchange of dialogue prayers between the presider and the people has taken place we have another one of those moveable parts of the Mass – the Prayer over the Offerings. Let's look at the dialogue first.

After washing his hands, the presider turns to the people and says;

> Pray, brethren (brothers and sisters),
> that my sacrifice and yours
> may be acceptable to the almighty Father.

Notice that once again, we are drawn to the fact that the people, deacon and presider are doing this together. It is our sacrifice, not his sacrifice. And it is a sacrifice that is being offered. It is a participation in the death of Christ through his Body and Blood. Not a repetition of a sacrifice once made, but a communion with the one and only sacrifice of Christ, made present in this community until he comes in glory.

The people respond;

May the Lord accept this sacrifice at your hands
for the praise and glory of his name
for our good
and the good of all his Holy Church.

The presider is our intermediary – it is he who stands in the place of Christ the head of the Church and speaks to his body, which is the Church. The sacrifice has three objects. The Mass is directed toward the praise of God and to glorify God for all God's works. It is offered for our good, that is, for the good of the community gathered at this particular Mass. Our greatest good is in coming to know and love God, for our human flourishing is achieved by this. Finally, it is for the whole Church.

We say the Church is holy, not as an expression of the collective holiness of the people. It is not as if the Church would lack holiness if its members failed to be holy. The holiness of the Church comes from the Holy Spirit who dwells in the Church and which may be compared to the soul of the Church (Lumen gentium 7). On the other hand, because the Holy Spirit does dwell in the Church, it would seem almost impossible to imagine that some and even many of her members would not in fact show signs of grace and holiness. When we proclaim a saint, we proclaim their holiness. There are far more uncanonised saints in the Church than canonised ones (officially recognised). Your nearest saint may be sitting in a seat near you at Mass. Or perhaps in your seat.

As soon as this dialogue is completed, the presider extended his hands over the offerings and prays a prayer over them. Each Mass has its own prayer over the gifts. These prayers will reflect the feast or season in which the celebration takes place. Let's sample a few to get a flavour of these. You can find them all if you have a daily Mass Missal.

Fifth Sunday of Lent:

> Hear us, almighty God, and, having instilled in your servants the teachings of the Christian faith, graciously purify them by the working of this sacrifice. Through Christ our Lord.

Fifth Sunday of Easter:

> O God, who by the wonderful exchange effected by this sacrifice have made us partakers of the one supreme Godhead, grant, we pray, that, as we have come to know your truth, we may make it ours by a worthy way of life. Through Christ our Lord.

Twenty-sixth Sunday in Ordinary Time

> Grant us, O merciful God, that this our offering may find acceptance with you and that through it the wellspring of all blessing may be laid open before us. Through Christ our Lord.

The people respond, Amen. In this way, they join their assent to the prayer which we have all said through the presider.

If you ponder just this short sample of prayers, you will notice the variety of ideas that each expresses. The prayer from Lent reflects that the season is one for renewed attention to learning and deepening our experience of faith through penance. In Easter, we have come to know that Jesus is the way and the truth by pondering the Paschal mysteries of his dying and rising and through baptism we have been immersed into the life of God. In Ordinary Time, we have this image of abundance, that all blessings will well up before us and enrich our lives.

There is so much richness to these very short prayers. Each week, it is a good thing to read the prayer for the following Sunday at some point, so that the language and content of it is more familiar to you as you hear it prayed. In this way, you can more fully join yourself to the prayer.

Presiders need to take care that they too are very familiar with the prayer so that they do not stumble over the form of the words (which in the current translation can sometimes be tricky). They should not rush over it as if it were just part of the dialogue before the Eucharistic prayer commences. We can all be enriched by attending to this little prayer.

32

Lift up your hearts

During the time of preparing the gifts of bread and wine we are also preparing ourselves. There is a lot of dialogue between the presider and the people from the time the gifts arrive at the altar to when the Eucharistic Prayer begins. We are building to a moment, a high point, the prayer of great thanksgiving or Eucharistic Prayer.

The presider asks us to 'Lift up your hearts'. We respond, 'We lift them up to the Lord'. Such a simple dialogue and yet so profound too. We reflected in earlier parts of this book that the heart in the ancient world is a metaphor for our entire being and for that which is most central to us, our core. We are being asked to 'lift up' the whole of what we are to God. In what sense do we mean to 'lift up'? In the context of the offering of the sacrifice of the Mass, it means to offer up ourselves, to join ourselves to the bread and wine to be offered to God. It is as if we are placing ourselves on the altar to be lifted up or offered to God.

Notice again that the language of 'we' not 'I' is used as we pray, 'We lift them up to the Lord'. It is a reminder of how profoundly linked we are to each other in the celebration of the Mass. Like the many grains of wheat and the many grapes that make the bread and wine, we who are many are made one in the Eucharist, through our sharing in communion with the Body and Blood of Christ.

St Paul reflects on this profound mystery in a number of places. To the Church of Rome, he writes, 'so in Christ we, though many, form one body, and each member belongs to all the others' (Romans 12:5). To the Corinthian Church, he writes, 'Is not the cup of thanksgiving for which we give thanks a participation in the blood of Christ? And is not the bread that we break a participation in the body of Christ? Because there is one loaf, we, who are many, are one body, for we all share the one loaf' (1 Corinthians 10:16-17). This last quote has been turned into a popular Eucharistic hymn sung in many parishes.

The action of lifting involves an act of the will. We are not passive but active in desiring and choosing to lift up our whole self to the Lord and in joining ourselves to the Eucharist. This little dialogue illustrates that active participation in the liturgy is not about having a job to do or having a special role to play or wearing special vestments. Each of us – presider, deacon and laity – is actively involved in offering the Mass and ourselves along with it. We see clearly that the whole Church is exercising its priestly ministry when we celebrate Mass. We are all lifting up the sacrifice.

When we gather for liturgy, we gather as the priestly people of God and each of us – bishop, presbyter, deacon and lay person – acts according to their priestly role in the assembly. The lay person and the deacon are not ordained priests but they are still anointed priests by virtue of baptism. All the Church, clergy and laity, participate in the common priesthood with Christ, through Baptism. Ordination as a priest (*sacerdos* in Latin) allows the one ordained to participate as Christ the head of the Church at the Eucharist but all the baptised participate as members of Christ's Body. Baptised people are not like the unbaptised people on the planet – the baptised are the priestly people of God and the Body of Christ, a holy nation.

Another important thing to attend to in this little dialogue is to recall that we are directing our worship to God. We are 'lifting up to the Lord'. While the Mass has a communal dimension and we do it in community, the focus is directed toward God. Our gaze is directed toward God and heaven, even as we know we are firmly rooted in the earth. God is not only the direction of our worship but the direction of our entire being and all aspects of our life. We are lifting up our heart, the core and totality of our being, toward God not only in the Mass, but as our life orientation.

Our work, our study, our family life, our marital life, our acts for justice and mercy, our way of relating to others, our sexual relations, our ways of speaking, our decisions about spending and saving, our decisions about consumption and care for the earth, our life in all its many and varied aspects, is to be voluntarily directed toward God. At least that is the ideal for which we strive and with God's grace in the Holy Spirit, we may one day achieve. We are lifting up all that we are, all that we have and possess, our entire will, toward God.

When we lift up our lives in the Mass, we do so with open hands. Open hands can give but they can also receive. We need to maintain a receptive posture and keep our hands and hearts and minds open to receive from God. When we give our lives over to God, if we keep our hands open, we allow God to transform the gift of our lives along with the gifts of bread and wine. Only God is ultimately able to transform us and work a Eucharistic miracle in us. We cannot transform ourselves through our own efforts. Joyfully lift up your hearts so that you can receive from the Lord more than we can ever ask or imagine. 'Glory be to him whose power, working in us, can do infinitely more than we can ask or imagine; glory be to Him from generation to generation in the Church and in Christ Jesus for ever and ever. Amen' (Ephesians 3:20-21).

33
Communion and being

I want to take a little side step and look not at the Mass but at two important concepts related to what we are doing there; religion and Church. Getting some renewed perspective on both of these terms can be important for developing a deeper understanding of the Mass. I have already suggested earlier that when we gather for Mass, *we are being Church* and not going to church. So, we need to shift a little our understanding of 'church'. Related to it is the word 'religion' and this word can cause all sorts of confusions and blockages for some. This is especially so when it is linked to terms like 'institutional religion' or 'organised religion'. Misunderstanding both words, I believe, can get in our way of being church.

Scholars who study this thing called 'religion' cannot agree on how to define it or what things to include and exclude from it. Some focus on doctrines, rituals and other markers as being distinctive of this thing called 'religion' and others are not so sure. Some include among the things called 'religion' Christianity, Hinduism and Judaism and others also include things like dogmatic atheism, belief in free-market capitalism, scientism, Marxism and much else besides.

Some people assume this thing called 'religion' is a distinct form of knowledge and belief that is entirely different from something called 'secular' knowledge and belief. Some people assume that the 'secular' is equated with the public or with society and that 'religion' with the private or special sub-sets within society. Others find such notions empirically unsupported and contested and of no real value in looking at human culture.

Quite commonly, people assume 'religion' means a set of doctrines, set of practices, a belief in God or gods or other supernatural agents, and distinctive rituals that are 'religious'. Again, commonly, people think that there are varieties of these things called 'religions' and even 'world religions' and that these varieties have always existed in some time or place. It sometimes surprises people to learn that terms like 'world religions' never existed until the twentieth century, that a 'religion' called Buddhism or one called 'Hinduism' is never mentioned by those names until the nineteenth century, and were terms never used by people who are said to be 'Buddhists' or 'Hindus'. In the seventeenth century, Muslims were considered by

Europeans as a Christian heretical sect and not a variety of 'religion'. The phrase 'the Christian religion' did not exist until the eighteenth century. What people quite commonly assume is, therefore, not necessarily true or not necessarily the way things have been or are. The concept of 'religion' is not found in any languages outside of Western European ones.

The idea that there are these things called 'religions' that can be defined by doctrines, rituals and other elements and which are subsets of the wider 'secular' society, comes to us from the 1750s. Essentially, the idea comes from a man called John Locke, who was not writing about 'religion' at all, but about the power of the Nation State. He invented the modern terms 'religion' and 'secular', more or less as described above. He defined it this way because he wanted to argue (in my very basic outline) that the Nation State was the great free association of individuals and it had power over all citizens as least as it concerned the public or secular sphere. The State had power over lesser associations like these things he called religions. A 'religion' was a free association of individuals who believed the same doctrines and agreed to worship in the same way. He said the State should allow these private associations to have their various doctrines and ways of worship as long as they kept it to the private sphere and they were not Catholic. Their doctrines had to be confined to the inner world of the believer and not things like should slaves be set free, should we go to war, should workers be paid just wages, should we care for the Earth and other public or 'secular' questions. Locke's starting point was politics but he did have some religious basis too. He saw in the Reformers' insistence on lists of doctrines and ways of worship as markers of true believers as a way of classifying these multiple groups of believers.

It was after Locke's time that we first see phrases like '*the* Christian religion' and Christianity being described as a 'religion'. Gradually during the nineteenth century, first Protestants and later Catholics, would use the term 'religion' more or less as Locke did. No Christian before him could ever have used such language or would have thought of himself as being a member of *the* Christian religion, or indeed any religion. It is from Locke's definition that we eventually get 'organised religion' and 'institutional religion'. Both of these terms are not helpful and don't tell us much about this thing called 'religion'.

Before Locke invented the terms 'religion' and 'secular', these had very different meanings. Religion meant one's public obligations, such as the obligation to respect one's parents, to observe special days, to commemorate the dead and heroes like on ANZAC Day or Veterans Day. Taking a public vow was religion because these were obligations we placed upon ourselves that could be attested to by others in society, i.e. in the public domain. That is why Catholics call sisters, brothers and presbyters who take public vows, religious, because they enter religion, in the pre-Lockean sense, of the public swearing of a vow.

Catholicism certainly – and Protestantism almost certainly – do not fit into the definition of this thing called a 'religion' (nor do any other of the 'religions'). If 'religions' are the things Locke means, and the general public means by 'religion' then they do not qualify. (By the way, 'Catholic*ism*' comes into use from the late nineteenth century in response to Catholics calling what Protestants believe, 'Protestant*ism*' earlier in that century.) I think the best working definition of Catholicism is 'a way of being for full human flourishing'. The doctrines, moral precepts, rituals and sacraments etc. are ways to form people in and give expression to this way of being for full human flourishing. There is a lot more I could say about that, but I don't have space here.

The other term is Church. The Catholic understanding of Church is rich and subtle. There is no single definition of Church. Multiple definitions, images and concepts need to all be held together, sometimes in tension with each other, to appreciate the complexity what Catholics understand by the term 'church.' Let's sample just some of this complexity.

One of the key documents of the Second Vatican Council is *Lumen Gentium*, the Dogmatic Constitution on the Church. In paragraph eight, we read:

> Christ, the one Mediator, established and continually sustains here on earth His holy Church, the community of faith, hope and charity, as an entity with visible delineation through which He communicated truth and grace to all. But, the society structured with hierarchical organs and the Mystical Body of Christ, are not to be considered as two realities, nor are the visible assembly and the spiritual community, nor the

earthly Church and the Church enriched with heavenly things; rather they form one complex reality which coalesces from a divine and a human element. For this reason, by no weak analogy, it is compared to the mystery of the incarnate Word. As the assumed nature inseparably united to Him, serves the divine Word as a living organ of salvation, so, in a similar way, does the visible social structure of the Church serve the Spirit of Christ, who vivifies it, in the building up of the body.

Notice how the Church is 'both and', not 'either or'. It is a community of faith, hope and love but is also a visible society. It is a structured, hierarchical organisation and it is also a mystical communion, the Body of Christ. There is not an institutional church separate from the mystical Body of Christ. There is not a sacramental reality from the Holy Spirit that is the Church, separate from the very human community with all its faults and failings. The Church of earth and the Church of heaven are co-mingled.

In *Lumen Gentium* paragraphs one to four, we learn that God intended that the Church would come into existence from the beginning of creation. That the Church was prepared for in the formation of the People of God, the Jews. That the Church reaches is fullest expression when Christ instituted it in his own lifetime and that the Holy Spirit constitutes the Church from moment to moment as in one prolonged epiclesis. That the Church is in Christ like a sacrament, a sign and instrument of communion with God and the unity of the whole of humanity. We are not saved alone but always in communion with others who are parts of me in the one Body of Christ. Church is not an optional extra to belief in Christ or faithful discipleship. We enter the Church, a communion, through the door that is baptism. The Church is the foretaste of the Kingdom of God which will be fully revealed when Christ comes again and the whole of creation is completed.

A person can pray alone and have her own level faith commitment and understanding and spirituality but she can never be fully Christian without remaining in the Body of Christ the Church. Something will always be missing because God did not call her alone, she was called as part of a Holy People the Church. Mass reconnects us with that Body and reminds us that we have companions on this journey as we go toward God together. This side of the coming of the Kingdom in its fulness, there is not going to be a perfect church, a perfect parish or a perfect celebration of the Mass, at least seen from the human dimension. Coming to Mass helps us to accept our own reality, we are being Church. Our full flourishing as humans comes from communion with God. Communion and being are intimately connected.

34

A mysterious exchange

We have encountered before a number of prayers that are prayed *sotto voce* (saying quietly). Some of these accompany rituals the deacon or presider perform during Mass. I don't know why the instruction is given for these to be prayed quietly. One of these *sotto voce* prayers concerns the preparation of the chalice.

The deacon (presider if there is no deacon) takes the chalice and pours in the wine and follows with a little water. As he pours a few drops of water into the wine, he prays (*sotto voce*);

> By the mystery of this water and wine may we come to share in the divinity of Christ who humbled himself to share in our humanity.

To get some context for this little ritual and its prayer, we need to look toward the Scriptures. First, we should look at St Paul's letter to the Church in Philippi (Philippians 2:5-11),

Have this mind among yourselves, which is yours in Christ Jesus, who, though he was in the form of God, did not count equality with God a thing to be grasped, but emptied himself, taking the form of a servant, being born in human likeness. And being found in human form he humbled himself and became obedient unto death, even death on a cross. Therefore, God has highly exalted him and bestowed on him the name which is above every name, that at the name of Jesus every knee should bow, in heaven and on earth and under the earth, and every tongue confess that Jesus Christ is Lord, to the glory of God the Father.

Secondly, there are many texts which speak of our transformation into Christ, because we have been baptised such as Romans 12:5, 'so we, though many, are one body in Christ, and individually members one of another'. 1 Corinthians 12:12, 'For just as the body is one and has many members, and all the members of the body, though many, are one body, so it is with Christ.' 1 Corinthians 12:27, 'Now you are the body of Christ and individually members of it'.

The text from Philippians is even more amazing because it applies a First Testament text about God the Father to Jesus, Isaiah 45:22-23;

'Turn to me and be saved,
all the ends of the earth!
For I am God, and there is no other.
By myself I have sworn,
from my mouth has gone forth in righteousness
a word that shall not return:

'To me every knee shall bow,
every tongue shall swear.'

What do we learn from this group of Scripture passages? First, we learn that God came among us as one like us in all things but sin. God took on human flesh and entered a fully human life with all that being human entails. In the person of Jesus, God humbles himself to enter our humanity and lives the life every human knows. He chose to be weak and vulnerable and subject to the powers of this world.

Secondly, we learn that through baptism we have entered into the Body of Christ, which is the Church and that we are parts of one another. In baptism, we have been immersed into the life of the Holy Trinity by sharing in Christ's life.

This a remarkable exchange of gifts. God comes into our human life so that our human life can be lifted up into the divine life. In the Eastern Catholic Churches and the Orthodox Churches, the name they give for this lifting up of our humanity into the divine life is *theosis*. *Theos* is Greek for God. *Theosis* then is our becoming one with the life of the Divinity.

As the water and wine co-mingle, so our life and the life of God should co-mingle. God comes to us so that we can go to God. God shares our life so that we can share God's life. In this simple little ritual and the prayer that accompanies it, we have such a profound theological reflection. Through the Mass, we recall that this is not a one-off offer. God did not come into our lives 2000 years ago through the incarnation and then leave us. God came into our life and remains in our life, constantly offering a renewal and transformation of our own life and constantly issuing an invitation to share in God's own life.

Holy Communion is more than receiving communion, in the form of bread and wine, it is also sharing in the communion of the Divine life, the life of God. You would be familiar with the children's game, hide and seek. The object of the game is about eventually being found or choosing to reveal one's self at the end when the searcher cannot find you. So it is with God. If God may seem hidden and mysterious from us, the object is still the same. God wants to be found and if we cannot find God then God will reveal God's own self. God once gave himself in the physical presence of Jesus, a real flesh and blood human being in a particular time and place, a Jew who spoke Aramaic and lived in what we know as Israel/Palestine today. The offer was not withdrawn with the ascension. God, in Christ, through the Holy Spirit is offered to us again and again.

May it be that as we come to accept this offer more deeply each day, we may come to share in the divinity of Christ.

35

Preface

You are likely to be familiar with a preface that one may sometimes find in a book. In the preface of a book the author outlines some of her aims and themes that may be encountered and other material that helps to orient the reader to what comes next. In the Mass, there is a preface before the Eucharistic Prayer. The Eucharistic Prayer (Prayer of Thanksgiving) is the one the presider says standing at the altar with arms raised. The preface comes after the dialogue about, 'Lift up your hearts'.

The preface at Mass is part of the Eucharistic prayer and much like the preface for a book it provides some orientation to what comes next and how we might relate this particular celebration of the Mass to the feast, season or occasion for which we have gathered. There is a variety of prefaces that may be used within a single season. There are two prefaces for use in Advent, a preface for the Feast of the Nativity (Birth of Christ), prefaces for Lent and Easter (Paschal Time), prefaces for Ordinary time, for the feast of saints, for the dead and for many other occasions. If you have a Missal, you can read them all. The presider will choose one from the appropriate season or feast. He may or may not tell the congregation which one he has chosen e.g. he may announce, 'Preface four of the Sundays in ordinary time'. The reason he would announce them is so that those following along in a missal can turn to the appropriate page and read along as he speaks or chants/sings the words.

Let us look at two examples. The first is taken from Preface VI of the Sundays in Ordinary Time:

It is truly right and just,
our duty and our salvation,
always and everywhere to give you thanks,
Lord, holy Father,
almighty and eternal God.

For in you we live and move and have our being,
and while in this body
we not only experience the daily effects of your care,
but even now possess the pledge of life eternal.

For, having received the first fruits of the Spirit,
through whom you raised up Jesus from the dead,
we hope for an everlasting share in the Paschal Mystery.

And so, with all the Angels,
we praise you,
as in joyful celebration we acclaim:

Holy, holy, holy…

The second is taken from Preface I of Easter

It is truly right and just,
our duty and our salvation,
at all times to acclaim you, O Lord, but

Easter Vigil: on this night
Easter Sunday: on this day

above all to laud you yet more gloriously,
when Christ our Passover has been sacrificed.

For he is the true Lamb who has taken away the
sins of the world;
by dying he has destroyed our death,
and by rising, restored our life.

Therefore, overcome with paschal joy, every land,
every people exults in your praise and even the
heavenly Powers,
with the angelic hosts,
sing together the unending hymn of your glory,
as they acclaim:

Holy, Holy…

You will notice that a preface always commences with the line, 'It is truly right and just, our duty and our salvation…' This is to underscore that the presider is praying this prayer in the name of the whole Church.

The last word of the dialogue before the preface has the people say, 'It is right and just'. And he is agreeing with this statement and joining our prayers together.

Next follows some version of words that indicate that what we are doing in offering the Mass, is a duty which is incumbent upon us. That is, we are called to proclaim Jesus' death and resurrection until he comes again, just as we are taught in Scripture. Everyone who has receive the sacraments of baptism, confirmation/chrismation and eucharist, is bound by this duty. At the same time as we fulfil this obligation we are also immersed in our salvation and what we do is for our salvation and that of the whole world. That's not a bad effort for a Sunday morning outing! We make present the mystery of our salvation every time we eat this bread and drink this cup. During the eucharistic prayer the presider will ask us to remind ourselves of this when he, not the deacon, proclaims; 'The mystery of faith'. The people respond with one of three responses, which the presider intones:

1. We proclaim your Death, O Lord, and profess your Resurrection until you come again.
2. When we eat this Bread and drink this Cup, we proclaim your Death, O Lord, until you come again.
3. Save us, Saviour of the world, for by your Cross and Resurrection you have set us free.

Each of the responses takes us to a variety of Biblical texts. The first two are related to the text of 1 Corinthians 11:26: 'For as often as you eat this bread and drink the cup, you proclaim the death of the Lord until he comes'.

The third refers in part to John chapter four and the encounter of the Samaritan woman at the well. For those who attend the Stations of the Cross during Lent, the second part of the response may be familiar to you, as it occurs there; 'We adore you, O Christ, and we bless you. Because by your holy cross you have redeemed the world'.

Any of the three can be used at any Mass but the third one is particularly apt for the season of Lent and therefore in some parishes it is only used during Lent, while the other two are used variously at all other times of the year.

After we mention that it is our duty and salvation, the prayer expands and provides a link to the season or feast we are celebrating by drawing our attention to something that is an aspect of this season or time. You can see this very clearly when you contrast the Ordinary Time Preface with the Easter Preface. The Easter one speaks directly about paschal or Passover time and the death and resurrection of Jesus.

All prefaces conclude with a lead into the Sanctus, the prayer that begins Holy, Holy, Holy. We will look at the Sanctus next.

In terms of your own preparation for Mass, it cannot often be known which particular preface from among the choices a presider has will be prayed at any Mass. The most that you can know is in Lent it will be chosen from among the Lent ones and at Easter from among the Easter ones and so on. You could perhaps study the appropriate range of prefaces for the times and seasons to at least become familiar with the kinds of themes and ideas that they suggest for the season.

36

Sanctus (Holy, Holy)

After the preface and immediately flowing from, it we begin to chant or say the Sanctus; 'Holy, Holy, Holy, Lord God of hosts'. Once again, we are reminded that what when we celebrate the liturgy, this is not only a gathering of the people in this church, but with the angel hosts of heaven, all the women and men who were baptised and have gone before us and all who are to be baptised. The whole Church of heaven and earth gathers when we gather for Mass.

The preface concludes with an invitation, 'And so with Angels, Archangels, with thrones and dominions and with all the hosts and powers of heaven, we sing the hymn of your glory, as without end we acclaim... Holy, Holy, Holy...' Heaven and earth is joined in this hymn and it is a hymn that we sing without ceasing. We should ponder this invitation. What we are doing has cosmic consequences. The unity of all things in space and in time is suggested by this invitation. Our voice today is part of an eternal today in which this hymn is chanted. We add our voice now to this hymn on earth and – God willing – we shall add our voice in the heavenly community too. You can tell your friends and family that today I sang with the angels! Even though the congregation may not have sounded like an angelic choir.

The text of the Sanctus – like so many of the texts of the Mass – comes either directly from Scripture or alludes to it. There are two direct references to Scripture in the Sanctus. The first part is directly inspired by Isaiah's vision of God's glory in Isaiah 6:1-3 (with an allusion to Daniel 7:10).

> *I saw the Lord sitting upon a throne, high and lifted up; and the train of his robe filled the temple. Above him stood the seraphim. Each had six wings: with two he covered his face, with two he covered his feet, and with two he flew. And one called to another and said, 'Holy, holy, holy is the Lord of hosts; the whole earth is full of his glory!'*

We have encountered this work glory (doxa in Greek) before. It refers to the Divine Presence among us. In the Sanctus, we acknowledge that God is present in all creation and in the entire universe, in heaven and earth. There is no place or time when God is not present and not holding all things in being.

> Holy, Holy, Holy Lord God of hosts.
> Heaven and earth are full of your glory.
> Hosanna in the highest.

The second part is a direct reference to the Gospel of Mark when Jesus enters the city of Jerusalem and is welcomed enthusiastically by a crowd waving branches and laying them and their cloaks in his path. 'Hosanna! Blessed is he who comes in the name of the Lord! Hosanna in the highest heaven!' (Mark 11:9-10). We commemorate this entry each year on Palm or Passion Sunday which opens Holy Week and the final days of Jesus leading to his death and resurrection.

Perhaps we can recall that moment in Jerusalem too, before we prepare ourselves to receive Jesus in the Eucharist. We may ask ourselves are we a fickle people, cheering and welcoming Jesus at the start of the week and then, if we tire or lose our way, does our enthusiasm wane? Do we join those who condemn him at the end of the week? Or are we like the apostles, who slink away and are not there to stand by Jesus at his crucifixion? When the going gets tough to live our faith and to witness to it, do we give up or slink away, hoping not to the noticed?

37

It is right and just

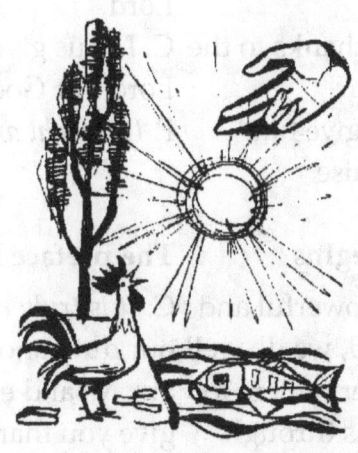

When the final translation of the Latin text of the Mass arrived in the English-speaking world in 2010, replacing the 'temporary' one from the 1970s, many found this phrase, 'It is right and just' a little odd sounding to our ears. We need to remember that these words were always in the Latin original but we translated them differently.

These words come from the dialogue between the presider and the people before the preface of the Eucharistic prayer is prayed. I have placed the 1970s translation in the left column and the 2010 translation in the right. 'C' is the celebrant or presider and 'P' is the people.

1970s translation-dialogue	**2010 translation - dialogue**
C. The Lord be with you.	C. The Lord be with you.
P. And also with you.	P. And with your spirit.
C. Lift up your hearts.	C. Lift up your hearts.
P. We lift them up to the Lord.	P. We lift them up to the Lord.
C. Let us give thanks to the Lord our God.	C. Let us give thanks to the Lord our God.
P. It is right to give him thanks and praise.	P. *It is right and just*.
The preface begins	**The preface begins**
C: Father, all powerful and ever living God, we do well always and everywhere to give you thanks through Jesus Christ our Lord…	C: *It is truly right and just*, our duty and our salvation, always and everywhere to give you thanks, Lord Holy Father, almighty and eternal God, through Christ our Lord…

Although the words themselves may be a little strange at first what is significant in the new translation – which is literal to the Latin at this point – is that the preface which opens the Eucharistic prayer begins with the presider echoing the words of the people. Through this verbal cue, the signal is given that the whole of the eucharistic prayer is our prayer, even though the words may be spoken by the presider. By 'our prayer' I mean the whole body of Christ, the laity, deacon, presbyter and bishop. We are all joined together in the offering of the Mass.

When we think back to earlier sections of the book, we know that the voice of the presider and people is also that of Christ who prays, *in*, *with* and *through* his Body the Church. Notice how the introduction to the Eucharistic prayer (the preface) reinforces this very point by saying that we are giving thanks (eucharist) *through* Christ our Lord. The whole of the Eucharist prayer is offered in the Holy Spirit through Christ to the Father, by all the people.

The phrase 'it is right and just' carries a sense of the expressions, 'this is as it should be' or 'this is necessarily so'. Giving thanks to God is not an external obligation imposed on us by Church law; nor is the giving of thanks confined to the great prayer of thanksgiving, called the Eucharistic (thanks giving) prayer. Giving thanks is a natural part of being a human being. Nothing else in creation can give thanks but us. We know we exist and we know the wonder of our creation. We know how much we have to be thankful for even if we don't always consider it or express some of these things in words.

We are thankful that there is something in the universe rather than nothing. The universe itself is so finely tuned. It expands at exactly the right rate, it contains exactly the right mix of chemical elements, it has gravity and that gravity has a very specific value and the size of the universe and the location of the Earth within it make it precisely a universe in which human life and our brains can exists. If any of these things varied in the slightest degree, we would not have a brain and our capacity to think and give thanks could not exist.

We can be thankful that we have life. We did not create ourselves; we are the product of the love and nurture of our parents. We did not educate ourselves and we are grateful to all the many teachers who enabled us to learn to read and write and who trained our minds for higher thinking that allowed some to learn trades or obtain higher education. We did not invent our own medications or perform our own surgeries or nurse ourselves back to health. We did not grow most of our food or prepare it for consumption. We are so utterly interdependent and vulnerable that we are caught in a vast lifelong web of receiving and giving. Thankfulness springs naturally from an acknowledgment of our dependence on others and the universe itself. Therefore, it is right and just to give thanks as a response to life and more so to the Author of Life.

Liturgy means the public worship acts of the Church. We have a duty as Christians to offer the Mass for ourselves and all people. This is a task the baptised are happy to take up on behalf of all the world. We pray for all Catholics, all other Christians, all people of all religious traditions and none. We offer the Mass for the saints and the sinners, for the sick and the well, for the righteous and the unrighteous. Christ died for all and we want to make the fruits of that sacrifice available to all so that all may have life and live.

To offer the Mass is also our salvation. Catholics do not believe that we can repeat or add to the sacrifice of Christ. When we celebrate Mass, we proclaim Christ's death and resurrection until he comes again. We make present now, and participate or have communion in, the one and only sacrifice of Christ. We are participating in our salvation.

Our attitude of thanksgiving is not confined to the Mass. We need to become the kind of people who give thanks always and everywhere through Christ our Lord. We need to acknowledge our thankfulness to so many people and for so many things. This acknowledgment reinforces our sense of mutual dependence and mutual vulnerability. Cultivating a thankful heart helps us become more fully human and more fully alive in Christ. There is no time in our life where we have not been dependent and vulnerable and we may have times when we are more dependent and vulnerable, whether this be at the start of life or its end. This is what it means to be human. This is why it is right and just to give thanks.

38

Great thanksgiving – Eucharistic Prayers

There are quite a lot of Eucharistic Prayers or Prayers of Great Thanksgiving. Four of them are mostly used on Sundays and, helpfully, they are known as Eucharistic Prayer I, Eucharistic Prayer II, Eucharistic Prayer III and Eucharistic Prayer IV. Throughout the year, presiders are encouraged to pray each of them as well as other Eucharistic Prayers in the Roman Missal. Sometimes Eucharistic Prayer I is required for a particular celebration. Each prayer has slightly different emphasis and may be more suitable during different parts of the year.

It is a pity when a presider only ever uses one or two of his favourite eucharistic prayers and does not draw on the treasury of the Church's prayer to enrich and deepen the faith of the people. Each of the Eucharistic Prayers has its own richness of theology and imagery to stimulate our faith and deepen our connection to the mystery that we celebrate.

The presider says these prayers at the altar, once the gifts of bread and wine have been prepared. For most of the prayer, he will pray with his arms extended in a gesture of thanksgiving and offering. In Australia, the people tend to kneel for most of this prayer but in some countries they stand. We need to learn to be attentive to the prayer for although the presider will say most of the words of this prayer, he is praying it in our name as the Body of Christ.

In order to prepare yourself to pray this payer with the presider and to stop your mind wandering, it is good to become familiar with the texts of each version of the Eucharistic Prayer. Each one has a preface that sets the scene for the prayer as it will unfold. The preface can vary according to the feast and season.

Each prayer includes some reasons for our giving thanks. These words orient us toward some aspect of the Paschal mystery. We can join with this prayer our own particular intentions.

Our prayer always acknowledges the wider dimensions of communion with God and our communion with all the baptised. We always pray for those gathered at the altar with us in this place. We always pray for and in communion with our diocesan bishop, who is the focus of unity for the local Church also called a diocese. We always pray for and in communion with the bishop of Rome (the pope) because he is a sign of the unity of the Church throughout the world. We pray in communion with the deacons and presbyters (clergy) of our diocese and all the people who share the name Christian. We are in communion with these other Christians, but not yet a perfect communion.

Our communion is wider even than the assembly of Christians on earth. We always pray with Mary, the Mother of God, Joseph her beloved spouse, the apostles and some of the martyrs and saints who may also be mentioned. If you listen carefully, the patron saint of the parish may be mentioned as well as any diocesan patron or other saint who may have significance in the life of the community.

We always include mention of those who have died. Sometimes, if there is a recent death or the anniversary of a death occurs, the presider may mention this person by name during the Eucharistic Prayer. They too remain part of the communion of the Church. Hopefully, the presider will pause briefly at the mention of the dead to give us a little time to call to mind our own deceased relatives and friends, particularly our parents.

Throughout each of the prayers, the word sacrifice and words which mean the same thing appear. The Mass is a participation in the sacrifice of Christ so we should expect to hear the language of sacrifice occur in this context which concerns the offering of the bread and wine which will become the Body and Blood of Christ. The Mass is not an additional sacrifice beside that of

Christ's sacrifice on the cross, it is a participation in that same sacrifice.

Praise is another theme that weaves its way through the Eucharistic prayers. The Mass is a sacrifice of praise to God. Praise and thanksgiving seem to belong to one another naturally. We praise God for the wonder of creation. We praise God for the gift of faith. We praise God for the life that comes to us through his Son who has overcome death.

During the eucharistic prayer and in our preparation to pray, it we should ponder some of these themes in our own life. How do I foster unity and communion in my world, among my family and friends and among colleagues? What things do I have to give thanks for? What are the blessings I have received? How do I take up my role as co-responsible with the clergy (and laity) for the mission of the Church? Do I truly value the place of the clergy in the life of the Church and the mission of the laity too? Are there saints and apostles whose story I need to know better and learn from? Do I sometimes have recourse to Mary the Mother of God and ask her to pray with me to her Son? Have I made time to remember my dead relatives and friends and prayed for them from time to time?

Above all, do I live with deep gratitude and thanksgiving in my heart for all the blessings I have received and give praise to God in good times and in bad, in sickness and in health, all the days of my life?

39

Send down your Holy Spirit

Catholics believe that Christ instituted the Church. The Church, which is his body, was intended by Christ to continue his presence and his work through her own life. The life of the Church is sustained and constituted by the power and presence of the Holy Spirit. By tradition, we speak of the day of Pentecost, and the outpouring of the Holy Spirit, as the birthday of the Church (Acts 2:1-13). The whole life of the Church from the time of Christ's ascension until now, and into the future, is sustained by a continual outpouring of the Holy Spirit. The Holy Spirit is, in a very real sense, to the Church what the soul is to the body (*Lumen Gentium* 4) it is the animating principle of her life.

Given this, it is no surprise that the Holy Spirit is central to the celebration of the Mass, and indeed all sacraments. During the Eucharist prayer the presider brings down his hands and extending them over the gifts of bread and wine he prays:

> 'Make holy, therefore these gifts we pray, by sending down your Spirit upon them like the dewfall, so that they may become for us the Body and the Blood of our Lord Jesus Christ.' (He makes the sign of the cross over them.)

This gesture of holding hands extended and calling down the Holy Spirit is called the epiclesis. The whole life of the Church is one prolonged epiclesis. The Holy Spirit pours out the life of grace to the Church and communicates Christs own life to us.

St Augustine reminds us that, as we are the Body of Christ, what is placed upon the altar, the gifts, are also a representation of ourselves. We are placed on the altar with the gifts. So, as we call down the Holy Spirit upon the gifts of bread and wine to make them the Body and Blood of Christ, so too we call the Holy Spirit down upon us that we may be transformed into what we are about to receive, the Body of Christ. We need to hear the words simultaneously transforming the gifts and us. We want to become more clearly the Body of Christ so that his work can continue visibly in the world.

I like the image of the dew fall. It seems to be such a gentle image and also a transformative image. Some mornings when I look out the window and see the dew on the grass and on the leaves of trees, the landscape seems to be softened and transformed. In the desert culture in which Judaism emerged, dew fall is important for sustaining life. That tiny little bit of moisture can sustain plant growth and allow shoots of fresh grass to grow in places of low rainfall. These grasses may support the small flocks the shepherds care for. Perhaps the Holy Spirit comes down upon us like the dew fall and sustains and nurtures our life in a similar way. When our faith may seem dry and arid and without life, this tiny gift of dew fall may sustain the finest shoots of life. New life can be sustained by the Holy Spirit even when it may appear to us that nothing is there.

Perhaps when we see the gesture and hear the words of the epiclesis, we might think of that beautiful anthem from Pentecost, 'Lord, send out your Spirit and renew the face of the earth'.

40

The Words of Institution

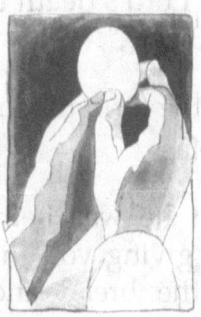

The Gospels of Matthew, Mark and Luke, along with the letter of St Paul to the Church in Corinth, each contain words through which Jesus instituted the celebration of the Eucharist. Each has some slight variations which are explained by the different points of emphasis found in each of the sources. We recall these words each time we celebrate the Mass and we call them the 'words of institution' or the 'institution narrative'. In the Mass, we use words from a combination of these narratives and in slightly different forms in each Eucharistic prayer.

Paul is our earliest known written source for the words Jesus uses at the Last Supper,

> For I received from the Lord what I also delivered to you, that the Lord Jesus on the night when he was betrayed took bread, and when he had given thanks, he broke it, and said, 'This is my body

which is for you. Do this in remembrance of me'. In the same way also the cup, after supper, saying, 'This cup is the new covenant in my blood. Do this, as often as you drink it, in remembrance of me'. For as often as you eat this bread and drink the cup, you proclaim the Lord's death until he comes. (1 Corinthians 11: 23-26)

You can see that the form of words is very similar to what we use in the Mass,

For on the night he was betrayed, he himself took bread, and, giving you thanks, he said the blessing, broke the bread and gave it to his disciples, saying:

Take this, all of you, and eat of it: for this is my body which will be given up for you.

In a similar way, when supper was ended, he took the chalice, and, giving you thanks, he said the blessing, and gave the chalice to his disciples, saying:

Take this, all of you, and drink from it: for this is the chalice of my blood, the blood of the new and eternal covenant; which will be poured out for you and for many for the forgiveness of sins. Do this in memory of me. (*Eucharistic Prayer III*)

Notice that there are four actions; he took, he blessed, the broke and he gave. First, the bread and a similar pattern follows with the cup. In the Greek language in which the Gospels and Paul's letters are written, the verbs, or the action words, convey a sense of a continuing action, not something in the past. Perhaps we need to hear this more like; taking, blessing, breaking and giving, so that we have a clearer understanding that Jesus is doing this now. We are not acting out a historical drama but something that Jesus is doing now, in and through the power of the Holy Spirit. Remember we are not repeating what Jesus did but we are participating in what Jesus does and continues to do.

We are reminded that Jesus was betrayed by one of his own. It is interesting that Christians have never hidden the fact that one of his chosen twelve, Judas, was to become his betrayer. It was not an outsider but one from his inner circle. In the Eastern Catholic Byzantine tradition (Liturgy of St John Chrysostom), the people recite a verse before receiving communion and in part of this verse they say,

> 'Accept me this day, O Son of God, as a partaker of Your Mystical Supper. I will not tell the Mystery to Your enemies, nor will I give you a kiss as Judas did, but, like the thief, I confess to you: Remember me, Lord when you come into your kingdom.'

We may wonder in what ways we have betrayed Jesus. How have we failed to live as he taught us? How have we as Church become a scandal and stumbling block, preventing people from coming to know Christ, and so betrayed him?

Receiving the eucharist as both bread and wine is a more complete experience of what it is that we are celebrating (Pandemic permitting). The documents on the liturgy, like the *General Instruction on the Roman Missal*, encourage sharing of the bread and the cup (when permitted and safe to do so) by all the people attending Mass. For most of the Church's history, the bread was received in the hand and the cup taken in the hands of the communicant. This too is more faithful to the institution narrative where Jesus hands out the gifts to his apostles to take in their hands. In most countries, the bishops have restored the practice of receiving in the hands.

When Moses came down from the mountain with the Law, they made an offering of animals,

> And Moses took half of the blood and put it in basins, and half of the blood he sprinkled against the altar. Then he took the book of the covenant, and read it in the hearing of the people; and they said, 'All that the Lord has spoken we will do, and we will be obedient.' And Moses took the blood and sprinkled it upon the people, and said, *'Behold the blood of the covenant* which the Lord has made with you in accordance with all these words' (Exodus 24:6-8).

This blood of Christ establishes a new covenant not only with the people of Israel, the Jews, but with all people. In the previous translation of the Mass, we said Christ's blood was poured out for *all* but now we say *many*. That is because the Greek word is many and not all. This does not change the fact that – as Scripture attests and the Church believes – Christ died for all, not just for this Christian group (2 Peter 3:9). God desires that all people come to know him and find salvation; how that might happen is known to God alone.

Finally, we need to consider this word memory. The Greek word used does not refer to a past event as if it is something in the past but to recall a past event as if it is still continuing in the present. In English, perhaps the closest 'memory' type word we have to this Greek word is nostalgia. When we experience nostalgia, we are not only recalling and remembering the past but we are experiencing the emotional memory and the vividness of the experience. When we are with old school friends remembering days in the school yard, it as if we can almost smell the stale vegemite sandwich in lunch boxes, as we recount some funny stories. We have a sense that we are not just recalling but we are there!

To do this in memory of Jesus is to do this as if we are gathered in the upper room with Christ and he is standing there and with his own hands is taking, blessing, breaking and giving to us in this very moment.

41

The Mystery of Faith

Immediately after the presider has concluded the words of the institution narrative, he genuflects in adoration and then says; 'The mystery of faith'. This is an invitation to proclaim what we believe that we are doing when we celebrate the Mass. The heart of the mystery is Christ's dying and rising again or the Paschal Mystery.

There are three acclamations that the people can make in response to this invitation and any one of them can be used with any Eucharistic prayer. As it is generally advised that the presiders make use of all of the various texts and their options throughout the course of the year, there needs to be some system of rotating the choice of acclamation. Perhaps one could be used throughout Ordinary time, another used for Easter and Christmas and the other for Lent and Advent.

The three possible acclamations are:

The Mystery of Faith

1. We proclaim your Death, O Lord and profess your Resurrection until you come again.

2. When we eat this Bread and drink this Cup, we proclaim your Death, O Lord, until you come again.

3. Save us, Saviour of the world, for by your Cross and Resurrection you have set us free.

The first two are similar in content and draw on 1 Corinthians 11:26, 'For as often as you eat this bread and drink the cup, you proclaim the death of the Lord until he comes'. We recall not only Christ's death and resurrection but his return and the completion of the world.

The third one draws on the Gospel of John. In chapter four, Jesus meets the Samaritan woman at the well and she tells all the people in her village about Jesus and this is where the term Saviour of the World is found. When the Samaritans return to Jesus after hearing the woman's testimony, they proclaim, 'It is no longer because of your words that we believe, for we have heard for ourselves, and we know that this is indeed the Saviour of the world' (John 4:42). This Gospel story occurs during the season of Lent and so perhaps it would be this acclamation that could be used during this season.

Many Catholics like to attend the Stations of the Cross throughout Lent and also on Good Friday morning. In the Stations ritual, there is a dialogue which also picks up similar language found in the third acclamation, 'We adore you, O Christ, and we bless you. Because by your holy cross you have redeemed the world'. This is said at each of the images of the Stations of the Cross as the people, or only some with the ministers, process by each Station. This may supply another reason for choosing the third acclamation during lent.

The whole of the Christian life is marked by the shape of Christ dying and rising. It is not only when we celebrate Mass. There are so many times when we strive to live as Christ taught us but we fail. There are so many times that life does not seem to work as we hoped. There are times when suffering, loss and disappointment enters into our life. The mystery of faith we acclaim at Mass can take us more deeply into the mystery of Christ's dying and rising and assist us to unite our life which that of Jesus. Perhaps when we experience these moments of doubt, of failure, of suffering we can pray. 'Lord Jesus, with you I will die and rise again'. Place these experiences on the altar with the gifts. Unite these experiences with the hope of the resurrection.

42

Great praise, Great Amen

The Eucharistic Prayers conclude with a beautiful acclamation of praise (doxology). The presider holds the paten and chalice up to show to the people. If there is a deacon. the deacon will hold up the chalice. If there are concelebrating priest but no deacon, only the presiding priest holds up the chalice and paten. As these are held up for the people to see, the presider chants or says,

> Through him, and with him and in him,
> O God, almighty Father,
> In the unity of the Holy Spirit,
> All glory and honour is yours for ever and ever.

The people respond, Amen.

The whole of the Mass is prayed through, with and in Jesus. It is Christ who is at prayer in his Body the Church. It is Christ who is the one offered in the Mass. It is Christ who is the one offering. It is the voice of Christ praying through the presider, deacon and people. It is Christ who speaks to them as well.

This is also the way Christian life should be lived; through him, with him and in him. We have been baptised into Christ and we seek to live such that the life of Christ in us becomes visible to all. There is no moment of our life that is not connected to Jesus in the Holy Spirit. The whole of our being and the whole of our doing should be a consecration to God because it is always lived in, through and with Jesus.

God is a communion of persons, Father, Son and Holy Spirit. We dwell in that communion through having been baptised into Christ. The trinitarian life of communion and love is a pattern of the Christian life. The Church is a communion of love. We have been baptised into Christ, and therefore we are parts of one another. We are always in communion with each other through Christ in the unity which the Holy Spirit brings about in the Church. We are the people who have been made one through the unity of the Father, Son and Spirit.

Our communion and unity are not a natural experience of community like a club or a political party. A club or political party membership comes from having a shared interest or shared values and beliefs, that is the result of natural desires we might have for unity in a common purpose. The communion that exists among us, as Church, is not an expression of our will or desire to be together in the way that we might choose to belong to a sports club or become a member of a political party. Our unity is an expression of God's will. God chose from the beginning that the Church would exist and it is created by baptism and the Holy Spirit.

Jesus prayed in the Gospel of John that we would remain one, just as the Father and Son are one. Our remaining in communion with each other through the gift of the Holy Spirit was so that God would be glorified and all people would come to believe in Jesus whom the Father had sent. In his final discourse to his disciples, Jesus prays;

> My prayer is not for them alone. I pray also for those who will believe in me through their message, that all of them may be one, Father, just as you are in me and I am in you. May they also be in us so that the world may believe that you have sent me. I have given them the glory that you gave me, that they may be one as we are one — I in them and you in me — so that they may be brought to complete unity. Then the world will know that you sent me and have loved them even as you have loved me. (John 17:20-24)

We are those who believe in him because of the message of the first disciples. It is for our continued unity that Christ prays.

The great Amen that the people may sing or say is not only in response to the final doxology but to the entire Eucharistic prayer. We are giving our assent to what the presider has prayed. We are making our own what was said in our name. We are joining ourselves to the Eucharistic prayer so that it is not only the words of the presider but also the words of the deacon and the people.

Sometimes it would be good to read through the whole of the Eucharist prayer that was used on a particular Sunday and to meditate on it slowly. If you have a Sunday missal at home, this is easy to do. Perhaps you could pause at the end of each section of the prayer and respond Amen. Make each section your own and affirm what is prayed in each section as your own, so that when you next pray the Great Amen at Mass you are fully aware of the whole of the Eucharistic Prayer that you are saying amen to.

St Teresa of Kolkata (Calcutta) once said that in acts of loving, especially for the poorest and most vulnerable, that we could make our lives something beautiful for God. If we make of our lives a beautiful gift to God through our love and compassion and devotion, then this is a form of giving glory to God through, with and in Jesus in the unity of the Holy Spirit.

43

Sharing peace

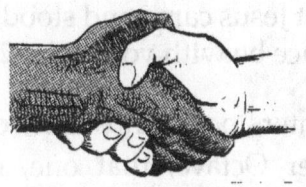

When a presbyter presides at Mass, he may begin with a greeting, 'The Lord be with you'. When a bishop presides at Mass, he begins with the greeting, 'Peace be with you'. The bishop stands in our midst as a living icon of Christ and these are the words that the risen Jesus uses when he greets the disciples. It is this context – of the risen Lord standing in our midst – that we recall when we come to the exchange of peace at Mass.

Every Mass is a celebration of the paschal mystery, Christ's dying and rising. Here, at this point of the Mass, just before we receive communion, we recall the presence of the risen Lord in our midst. In the Gospel of John, we appreciate the importance of peace in the encounter between Jesus, now risen from the dead, and those whom he meets.

> On the evening of that day, the first day of the week, the doors being shut where the disciples were, for fear of the Jews, Jesus came and stood among them and said to them, 'Peace be with you'.
> John 20:19

> Jesus said to them again, 'Peace be with you. As the Father has sent me, even so I send you'. John 20:21

> Eight days later, his disciples were again in the house, and Thomas was with them. The doors were shut, but Jesus came and stood among them, and said, 'Peace be with you'. John 20:26

These encounters occur in what we celebrate as the Paschal or Easter Octave, that one, eight-day period through which we prolong the celebration of Easter Sunday.

Peace occurs as a theme throughout the Gospel of John. It is worth attending to another passage before we look at the prayers of the Mass.

> Peace I leave with you; my peace I give to you; not as the world gives do I give to you. Let not your hearts be troubled, neither let them be afraid. John 14:27

> I have said this to you, that in me you may have peace. In the world you have tribulation; but be of good cheer, I have overcome the world. John 16:33

When we read these texts, we have to recall that, although in the narrative of the Gospel they occur before the events of the death and resurrection of Jesus, the Gospel itself is written after these events and so we still hear the voice of the risen Lord speaking to us. Jesus is offering a peace that is different from the ordinary peace that the world offers. The world offers a peace that is the absence of conflict, but the peace of Christ is more than this.

The peace of Christ speaks to our hearts, to the inner core of our being and our essential orientations. His peace lets this inner core become untroubled and offers deep calm amidst the passing troubles of this world. The Greek word for world (*cosmos*) that John uses here in 16:33, is his way of saying a place of chaos and disorder and sin and evil and going astray. The peace he gives belongs to the world of order, new orientation, beauty, gracefulness and virtue which overcomes and triumphs over the disordered world.

Chapter 16 of John is part of Jesus' discourse to his disciples about his death and rising. Although they do not know it yet, they are about to enter what for them will seem like their very darkest day when all hope is lost – Good Friday. Yet Jesus will overcome death and offer new life to all.

If we have this context in mind, we can turn our attention to the prayers of the Mass at the exchange of peace.

Sign of Peace

> P: Lord Jesus Christ,
> who said to your Apostles;
> Peace I leave you, my peace I give you;
> look not on our sins,
> but on the faith of your Church,
> and graciously grant her peace and unity
> in accordance with your will.
> Who live and reign for ever and ever.
> C: Amen.

P: The peace of the Lord be with you always.
C: And with your spirit.

If appropriate, the Deacon, or the Priest, adds:

P: Let us offer each other the sign of peace.

The prayer is addressed to Jesus and uses two titles attributed to him; Lord and Christ. Immediately, the prayer takes us to the context in the Bible where Jesus shares his peace with the apostles and in a sense addresses us too. The peace that we are talking about in this prayer is not just some form of greeting but is a gift Jesus himself gives to us. Not any kind of peace but the kind we saw above.

We acknowledge that we, the Body of Christ the Church, have sinned. We address our first petition to ask that the Lord Jesus Christ does not focus his attention on our failings but looks instead to the faith. That faith includes our conviction that our sins are forgiven. This is followed by a second petition that the Lord Jesus Christ graciously grant to the Church peace and unity. We have seen that the kind of peace Christ wills for the Church is that deep and abiding peace which is confident that the world is overcome and that good will ultimately triumph.

Christ also wills that the Church maintain its unity, a unity sadly broken by the will of women and men, who have allowed division and discord to enter the Body of Christ. To this day, Christians remain divided into Catholic, Orthodox and Protestant communities. Sometimes within these communities, other divisions also form and are maintained. Even within parishes, discord and disunity can occur.

> Jesus prayed to the Father in the last supper discourse, 'I do not pray for these only [the apostles], but also for those who believe in me through their word, that they may all be one; even as you, Father, are in me, and I in you, that they also may be in us, so that the world may believe that you have sent me'. John 17:20

Christ's will for us is to share in the unity he shares with the Father. Our sharing in this unity is to be a sign and sacrament of the unity of the whole human race. Maintaining unity among Christians is essential to the effective proclamation of the Gospel. Some outside the Christian community, correctly, point to our disunity and find our preaching of love and unity not very credible.

The rite of exchange of peace can end with the words, 'And with your spirit'. It is not essential that the people exchange a sign of peace among themselves. The presider has already prayed for our peace and unity and we responded with our amen of agreement.

When the deacon – or presbyter if there is no deacon – invites us to exchange a sign of peace, this is not a general greeting or a hello to each other. We need to be conscious that we are sharing the peace of Christ and his desire for unity as we have seen above. Normally, the greeting is exchanged in a manner that is suited to the local culture and custom. It should not be a greeting to everyone present but a sober greeting and exchange of the peace of Christ with those immediately near us. As we exchange the peace, try to be aware of the risen Christ speaking his words of peace and urging us to be one as the Father and he are one. Exchanging the sign with just a few people near us may help us be recollected and mindful of the deep significance of this little ritual.

44

Praying as Jesus taught us

The Gospels contain two versions of the Lord's Prayer. The Gospel of Luke has a much shorter one than Matthew. The one from the Gospel of Matthew is the version we use at Mass (below in the *Revised Standard Version*).

> Our Father who art in heaven,
> Hallowed be thy name.
> Thy kingdom come,
> Thy will be done,
>   On earth as it is in heaven.
> Give us this day our daily bread;
> And forgive us our debts,
>   As we also have forgiven our debtors;
> And lead us not into temptation,
>   But deliver us from evil. (Matt 6:9-13)

We stand to say this prayer, perhaps because we are addressing God directly and also because the words we use are those which Jesus gave us. In many of the pagan religions surrounding the ancient Jews, ordinary people, but not priests, would often approach the gods on their knees or fully bowed down. Jews, in contrast, would often stand to deliver prayers with arms outstretched, much as we see the clergy do during the Lord's prayer. In some countries, the people also pray the Lord's prayer with arms raised in a similar fashion to the clergy.

As with so much of the language of the Mass, it is the plural voice that we use – 'our' and 'us' – not the singular 'I' and 'me'. We have a common Father and we are, therefore, sisters and brothers to one another. We address God with the familiar and even intimate term of Father. This does not mean Christians believe God is a male. If this were the case then what would we make of references to God as an eagle, a shade in the desert or pool of cool and refreshing water or a rock or mother, all of which are found in the Bible? Father, or Abba in Aramaic, is Jesus' most characteristic way of addressing God and his relationship as Son is unique.

The expression 'in heaven' does not mean that God is not close to us but that God is ultimately unknown to us and not visible to us and is not to be identified with anything in the material world. In the pagan world surrounding the Jews of Jesus' day, things like the wind, sun, eagles and storms were gods or part of the spirit world. In the Jewish way of thinking, these things were all part of creation and God was their creator.

Hallowed means to make or be holy. God has no name. When we use names for God, like Father or Mother or Rock or Saviour in the Bible, these are all metaphors. The sacred name of God in Hebrew is represented by the equivalent English letters YHWH, without any vowel indicators, and therefore it cannot be pronounced in Hebrew. Often times, the YHWH is replaced with *Adonai*, which is like Lord. Sometimes, YHWH in every day speech is replaced with the Hebrew *Ha Shem* (The Name). Christians, but not Jews, in the 18th century made up a pronunciation for YHWH by inserting the vowels from Adonai to create 'Yahweh'. This is not a Hebrew word or any word actually. Out of respect for our Jewish sisters and brothers and for the original intention of the Bible, Christians are asked to no longer use this word in Bible translations, hymns and prayers. Catholics stopped this practice only in the close of the twentieth century.

We pray for the coming of the Kingdom of God. Announcing the arrival of the Kingdom is central to Jesus' message. This is not a work of human hands nor is a social justice project, whereby through our efforts we eliminate all injustices. It is the elimination of all injustice, but is much more than that too. It is when God will create a new heaven and a new earth and when we shall see God. It is the completion of all history and all creation.

We pray for a complete alignment between heaven and earth, so that God's will directs all things. If heaven represents the complete fulfilment of God's will, then we are praying that the earth will be transformed. We could begin this alignment with deciding to commit ourselves to living as God wants us to live.

The petition for daily bread can direct us toward focusing on what is essential. Our daily needs for food and drink and shelter need to be attended to, but we should not become focused on tomorrow or accumulating more and more. We need to ask ourselves if we have set our heart on treasure that lasts, the virtues that lead to God and full human flourishing, or on treasures of this world that will fade and rust. What have we set our hearts upon?

We set for ourselves a standard of forgiveness we should expect from God and from other people. If we are reluctant to forgive others and if we hold their faults and failings against them, why should we expect something that we are not prepared to give? Forgiveness – both the giving of it and sometimes the receiving – can be hard. Forgiveness liberates those who forgive and those who are forgiven.

God is not going to lead us toward temptation so this petition needs to be understood in the light of other teaching on temptation in the Bible and the tradition of the Church. In this sense, God guards us from temptation and provides us with the grace of Christ to strengthen us against temptation. As our guard and shepherd, God keeps watch over us, and protects us from dangers. The shepherd, knowing and area where foxes or wolves may inhabit, will not lead us there or let us stay there. God is the Shepherd of Israel and also of the New Israel, the Church. If we follow the path the Good Shepherd has made for us, we will not stray into dangerous territory.

We will be delivered from the evils that may be there and find the way of virtue and of life.

The Lord's prayer offers us a summary of the Gospel. It is fitting that we recall this Gospel just before we are to come to the time of Holy Communion. We will have a taste of the goodness of the Kingdom when we come forward to receive the bread and wine of the Eucharist.

45

Behold the Lamb of God

Almost at the very beginning of the Gospel of John, John the Baptist sees Jesus walking toward him and announces to all who are near, 'Behold, the Lamb of God, who takes away the sin of the world!' (1:29) Later in the Gospel of John, Jesus will gather for the Last Supper not on the day of Passover ° as happens in Matthew, Mark and Luke ° but before it. He will die upon the cross on the day of preparation when all of the lambs are slaughtered for the feast of Passover. This is not some error on John's part; he is trying to interpret the death of Jesus in the light of this important Jewish festival.

On the day leading up to Passover, the Day of Preparation, all the lambs for the Passover meal are slaughtered and everyone goes to the temple to get their lamb. In Jerusalem, in Jesus' time, this would have meant thousands of lambs being slaughtered. And in John's Gospel, that's the day on which Jesus is crucified. The dramatic scene in John's gospel has Jesus hanging on the cross while the lambs are being slaughtered for Passover. We are asked to think of Jesus as a Passover lamb.

Passover is an English word for *Pesach* (Hebrew) which in Latin became Paschal and hence the Easter season is Paschal or Passover time. This annual Jewish festival commemorates the liberation of Israel from slavery in Egypt recounted in the Book of Exodus. We read this story every Paschal Vigil on Holy Saturday night. Each Jewish family gathers, sometimes with other families, to share a sacred meal in their home. They share a Passover/Paschal Lamb, bread and wine, among other things. This is the context for the Last Supper in the other Gospels. John keeps the Passover focus but shifts the focus to the Lamb.

Just before we receive communion, there are a number of small rites within the communion rite. The first of these is the fraction rite, where the larger host is broken into small pieces for consumption. Then an even smaller piece is broken off and dropped in the consecrated wine. As the presider does this, he prays, 'May this mingling of the Body and Blood of our Lord Jesus Christ bring eternal life to us who receive it'.

As the rite of fraction continues, the people begin to chant the following:

> Lamb of God, you take away the sins of the world,
> have mercy on us.
> Lamb of God, you take away the sins of the world,
> have mercy on us.
> Lamb of God, you take away the sins of the world,
> grant us peace.

We use the same words John the Baptist used when he recognised Jesus coming toward him. We recognise him and then we ask him to have mercy on us and then to grant us peace. We profess Jesus to be our Passover Lamb and we recognise that he does more than liberate us from slavery in Egypt – he liberates us from sin and from death.

When the rite of fraction is complete and the people have ceased the chant, the presider holds up the host over chalice and directs our gaze toward the gifts which he now refers to as 'the Lamb'. In the Eastern Catholic Churches, the square of bread that is to be consecrated and which was cut from the round loaf, is also called the Lamb. We gaze on Christ who is the Passover Lamb for us and who passed over from death to life at Easter (Pascha).

The words that accompany this gesture echo the words of the congregation who have already chanted their recognition of the Lamb of God.

Behold the Lamb of God,
behold him who takes away the sins of the world.
Blessed are those called to the supper of the Lamb.

We don't use 'behold' very much these days. It means not only to observe but to look upon something that is impressive or significant. We might say, 'It was a pleasure to behold that beautiful sunset,' or 'the vast crowd that had gathered for the event was a sight to behold.' We are meant to gaze with wonder and awe at the Lamb as it is held up for us. God has come among us in the humble form of this bread and this wine. That is a sight to behold! This is Jesus, who takes away the sins of the world.

Occasionally, I have heard a presider say in error, 'blessed are *we*' and not 'blessed are *those*' who are called to the supper of the Lamb. 'We' refers to the people who are gathered at this Mass but 'those' refers to all who have been and will be baptised. This is a group that transcends the assembly in a parish church. We should be aware of this much larger group that also includes the company of saints and angels.

Many scholars believe that there is a connection between the community that gave rise to the Gospel of John and the community that gave rise to the Book of Revelation. One of the common themes is the constant identification of Jesus with the Lamb of God throughout. Indeed, the second part of the phrase that the presider prays when holding up the Lamb for us to behold is adapted from this book, 'Blessed are those who are invited to the marriage supper of the Lamb.' (Revelation 19:9)

There are so many references to the Lamb in Revelation that just a few will take us closer to the image of the Lamb and the Mass. The Church is frequently referred to as the Bride of Christ in the Second Testament. In this passage from Revelation, the marriage image is clear, 'Let us rejoice and exult and give him the glory, for the marriage of the Lamb has come, and his Bride has made herself ready' (Revelation 19:7). We, the Church, gaze on the Lamb who is the groom at our wedding.

We are also reminded that in the Book of revelations all the company of saints and martyrs standing before God and the Lamb at the altar chanting aloud, 'Worthy is the Lamb who was slain, to receive power and wealth and wisdom and might and honour and glory and blessing!' (Revelation 5:12). As we behold the mystery before us, we unite our voices with this company in singing the same praises.

All those who have been baptised once were robed in white, as the clergy and altar servers are now robed in white as a reminder of our baptism. 'After this I looked, and behold, a great multitude which no one could number, from every nation, from all tribes and peoples and tongues, standing before the throne and before the Lamb, clothed in white robes, with palm branches in their hand...' (Revelation 7:9). There are Christians today from almost evert tribe and people and language. In countries like Australia, many of our parishes witness to the ethnic and cultural diversity of the Church.

Take some time to gaze and to behold the deeper meaning as we see the Lamb lifted up before us.

46

A believer's prayer

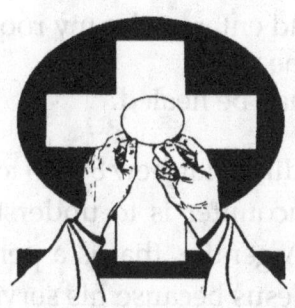

As we have seen several times in this reflection on the Mass, the texts and gestures of the Mass are frequently taken directly from Scripture or reference or adapt scriptural texts. Just before the people receive communion, the presider holds up the chalice and host to the people and says;

> Behold the Lamb of God,
> behold him who takes away the sins of the world.
> Blessed are those called to the supper of the Lamb.

As we saw previously, this text is drawn from the Gospel of John. The response of the people is adapted from Matthew 8:5-13 and verse 8 in particular; 'But the centurion answered him, "Lord, I am not worthy to have you come under my roof; but only say the word, and my servant will be healed"' (Matthew 8:8).

When the people respond at Mass the text of the Gospel is only slightly adapted so that the focus becomes each one of us praying it. We say *'my soul'* instead of my servant.

Lord, I am not worthy
that you should enter under my roof,
but only say the word
and *my soul* shall be healed.

It is worth reading Matthew 8:5-13 to understand how important this encounter is to understanding what we are saying now. A gentile, that is a person who is not a Jew, approaches Jesus because his servant is ill. Not just any gentile but a high-ranking soldier in the Roman army, which was the occupying force in Israel at the time. Jews should not enter the house of a gentile, in those days, and so the centurion says to Jesus, 'Sir (Lord), I am not worthy to have you under my roof (that is, in my home); just give the word and my servant shall be healed'.

Jesus is astonished at what he hears, because this gentile expresses such great faith in him. The centurion knows his servant will be healed just by Jesus' will and not by his presence to effect a healing. Jesus says, 'I tell you solemnly, nowhere is Israel (*that is, among his own people*) have I found faith like this'.

When we pray these same words – although slightly adapted to the situation of Mass – we too are professing our faith in Jesus. We are professing our faith in Jesus and acknowledge that the participation in the eucharist is food for our healing. It is not a question of our being worthy or not, Jesus comes to us in his Body and Blood to heal us of sin and restore us to wholeness.

Sometimes when people hear this little prayer they focus on the unworthy part. It is true that we are not saved because we make ourselves worthy of it. Salvation is always an unmerited gift. The prayer itself has a focus on affirming our faith in Jesus as saviour and healer. It is foremost a believer's prayer and an affirmation of faith not a profession of our unworthiness or lowliness. We are professing our faith in Jesus' capacity to make us whole.

It is worth pondering this little believer's prayer. Do we truly believe, deep down, that Jesus will lead us to wholeness? Jesus is not only fully God but also fully human. In learning to trust more in Jesus and his word, we learn to be more fully human and to live the life God intended for all human beings. We might also consider the ways in which we are not fully flourishing as a human being. Where are the fault lines, where are the failings that limit us from becoming fully human and fully alive? If we are honest with ourselves and acknowledge the parts of our life that need healing and restoration, we can then know what we are asking for when we profess our faith in Jesus' capacity to heal and make whole.

Without some degree of self-reflection, we may delude ourselves into thinking that we are self-sufficient and do not need healing or indeed need God. Learning to express our faith in Jesus to lead us to wholeness is also expressing our trust in him. The centurion has come out from his home and his servant is back there, yet he trusts and is confident that Jesus' will to heal will achieve its purpose. He does not need to return home to verify the healing. There is implicit trust in Jesus that this will be done.

At this moment in the Mass, we are about to approach Jesus in the eucharist but at the same time we express our trust that what we are about to receive will be for our healing. We feel it in our bones that our faith is not misplaced. We may think of the words of the prophet Isaiah, 'By his wounds we are healed'. For the one we are to receive, the Risen Lord, is the one who still bears in his body the wounds inflicted on him in his death, as Thomas attests (John 20:24-28). With Thomas, we can profess. 'My Lord and my God'. At this moment, we make a believer's prayer from our heart.

47

Corpus Christi procession

I still have memories – from when I was in primary school – of participating in *Corpus Christi* processions on *Corpus Christi* (Latin for the Body of Christ) Sunday. We would parade around the local streets outside the cathedral with the Blessed Sacrament carried in a monstrance, under a kind of canopy with four poles, with a man on each corner. The clergy would lead us and the laity follow behind singing eucharistic themed hymns like 'Soul of My Saviour' and 'Sweet Sacrament Divine'. I wondered what our Protestant neighbours and those of no faith at all made of this very external ritual of our Catholic eucharistic faith.

The Solemnity of The Body and Blood of Christ – as it is now called – occurs on the second Sunday after the Paschal (Easter) season ends. That is, two Sundays after the festival of Pentecost. Some parishes still have a public procession of the Blessed Sacrament to mark the occasion and, in some dioceses, one combined procession may be organised. As important as such processions may be to nurturing eucharistic devotion and emphasising the real presence of Christ in the eucharist, it should not distract us from the weekly corpus Christi procession that occurs in every Mass each Sunday.

In the Second Testament, the term body of Christ refers to Jesus' physical body and also his body the Church. Matthew, Mark and Luke each included in their Gospel an account of the Last Supper which has a version of the words we use at Mass; Jesus explicitly refers to his body at the Last Supper; 'Now as they were eating, Jesus took bread, and blessed, and broke it, and gave it to the disciples and said, "Take, eat; this is my body" (Matthew 26:26). He does not say take this as a symbol of my body or as a metaphor of my body but uses the word for his flesh. This is my body. Paul also uses similar words in his letter to the Church at Corinth, 'This is my body which is for you. Do this in remembrance of me. (1 Corinthians 11:24).

What we receive in the eucharist is the Body and Blood of Christ, though it appears in the form of bread and wine. Jesus, the Christ, gives his own body for us. The life given on the cross is now given in the eucharist.

We take and receive Jesus himself and he transforms us into what we receive – the Body of Christ.

Throughout the Second Testament, the Body of Christ has another meaning. The Body of Christ is also the Church. We only need to look at a selection of the many references to the Church as the Body of Christ to get the rich sense of this expression.

> 'For just as the body is one and has many members, and all the members of the body, though many, are one body, so it is with Christ. For by one Spirit, we were all baptised into one body—Jews or Greeks, slaves or free—and all were made to drink of one Spirit.' 1 Corinthians 12:12-27

> 'So, we though many, are one body in Christ, and individually members one of another. Romans 12:5

> 'Now you are the body of Christ and individually members of it.' 1 Corinthians 12:27

> 'God has made him (Jesus) the head over all things for the church, which is his body, the fulness of him who fills all in all.' Ephesians 1:22-23

> He is the head of the body, the church; he is the beginning, the first-born from the dead, that in everything he might be pre-eminent. Colossians 1:18

We who are baptised are baptised into the Body of Christ and are parts of him and of one another, because we have all been made one in the same body. Each time that we stand up and make our way toward the minister of communion, we form and take part in a corpus Christi procession. It is the body of Christ moving forward to receive the Body of Christ, in order that it may become more fully that which it receives.

At this part of the Mass, hymns should be sung as soon as the presider has taken communion and the *corpus Christi* procession forms until the *corpus Christi* procession has ended. Just as it is with the *Corpus Christi* procession around the outside of the Church, so too with the *corpus Christi* procession that occurs every Mass. The hymns are always and only those that sing of the Body of Christ, the Eucharist and receiving communion. This is, it is not a time for singing favourite hymns like the 'Peace Prayer of St Francis', or 'How Great Thou Art' or 'Amazing Grace' or any other hymn that does not focus on the eucharist and communion. The hymns are meant to accompany the action of the whole body of Christ, the Church, participating in communion with Christ and each other through sharing in the bread and wine.

It is best if communion is offered under both kinds, bread and wine. Sometimes there are good reasons for restricting access to the cup, like during a pandemic, but at all other times, and especially on Sundays both should be offered to the people so that the fullest participation in the sign of communion is available to all. The diocesan bishop provides the permission for parishes to offer both at every Mass.

During communion time, we can focus our attention on the Body of Christ, the Church, as we process to receive the Body of Christ, which is Jesus the Lord. It is an opportunity to reflect on the fact that these women and men and children passing by me and walking with me are a part of me. We are each part of the one body in Christ. The profound mystery of his Body which is the Church should not be lost as we make our own way to receive his Body and Blood in the eucharist. We need to be conscious of our walking with this pilgrim people, sharing the same journey of faith. Deeply aware that all of these women and men, in their many ages, shapes, colours, languages, ethnicities and abilities, are truly each a part of me and I of them. Together, each week, we form this little *corpus Christi* procession to remind ourselves of who we are, as we are on the way to meet the Lord together.

48

What is it that you say Amen to?

> *If you, therefore, are Christ's body and members,
> it is your own mystery that is placed on the
> Lord's table! It is your own mystery that you are
> receiving! You are saying 'Amen' to what you
> are: your response is a personal signature,
> affirming your faith. When you hear 'The body of
> Christ', you reply 'Amen'. Be a member of
> Christ's body, then, so that your 'Amen' may
> ring true!*
>
> St Augustine, Sermon 272

It seems like such a simple verbal exchange. The communicant looks at the minister of communion and the minister says, as she or he holds up a consecrated host before the communicant, 'The Body of Christ'. The one to receive communion simply says, 'Amen'. In all, just five simple words. Yet how profound is this simple exchange.

There are three ways to look at what the communicant is saying Amen to in this brief exchange from the perspective of the one receiving communion. First, she is saying Amen to the minister of communion who recognises that the communicant is part of the Body of Christ. The second is to the mystery which is before her eyes, that the bread and wine have become the Body and Blood of Christ. The third is to the Body of Christ that she is becoming because she is being transformed into the body of Christ the Church. Let's look at each of these three ways of pondering that, Amen.

We believe that when we are baptised, we are baptised into the Body of Christ which is the Church. We can only come forward to receive communion because we have been fully initiated into this Body through baptism, chrismation/confirmation and first Holy Communion. These are the three sacraments of Christian initiation for all Catholic (Eastern and Western) and all Orthodox Christians. Lay Christians are not somehow defined by being not ordained, that is by what they are not, as if the two significant categories in the church are those ordained and those not.

Lay people, which includes catechumens (those preparing to be baptised), are an order in the Church. They are different from all other women and men on the planet because they are part of the Body of Christ which is the Church. Order simply refers to the place where one stands in the body of the Church. Together, the clergy and laity constitute the one Body of Christ and together they are the People of God. So, with that 'Amen' we acknowledge what the minister sees, that we are indeed part of the Body of Christ.

In the second sense in which we use 'amen' we are affirming two realities at once. We affirm that when Christ said, 'this is my body, this is my blood', we indeed share in his very self. This is no mere symbol but the reality of Christ which we receive. Catholic and Orthodox Christians believe this to be true as a matter of faith. Some Protestants have some sense of what we call the real presence but for others the bread and wine are merely symbols of Jesus' last meal with his friends. Catholics and Orthodox affirm the reality of Christ truly present in the Eucharist.

The second reality we affirm in the second sense of 'Amen' is the reality that the Eucharist makes the Church. Catholic and Orthodox Christians believe that the Church is most fully herself when the bishop is gathered with the presbyters, deacons and laity in one common celebration. Because of the size of dioceses and eparchies, it is actually not possible today to have everyone at the same liturgy, but in the Second Testament era and the first three centuries of Church life this was a very real possibility. Nonetheless, we always celebrate the Mass in communion with our bishop and through him the whole local Church. We always mention the diocesan bishop or eparch in the Eucharistic prayer. Catholics, both East and West, will also include the name of the current Bishop of Rome to emphasise the communion of the whole Church throughout the world. The eucharist literally makes the Church come into visible existence by gathering all the people around the altar.

The third sense in which we say 'Amen' is to the reality that we are becoming. The Church is made up of saints and sinners, and as such is always in the process of becoming the Body of Christ. Perhaps a better way to say it is the whole Church is on pilgrimage in time and we are moving toward the Kingdom of God in its fulness. While on that journey, we see dimly as in a partly polished mirror a blurry image of what we are to be, the Body of Christ. If you have ever seen your face reflected in a stainless-steel pot lid, that is the kind of image St Paul has in mind, when he says that now we see dimly but when Christ is fully revealed we shall see things as the truly are (1 Corinthians 13:12).

We need to come back week after week to receive eucharist because this is the food that makes us become truly what we are. In another one of his sermons, St Augustine compares the difference between ordinary food and the food that is the eucharist. When we eat ordinary food, we transform it into our own bodies by absorbing it and feeding our hungers and giving us strength as well as food for our growth. That is, we transform the food into what we are. With the food of the eucharist, the process is reversed. We are transformed by what we eat, the Body and Blood of Christ, so that we become what we eat, the Body of Christ the Church. Jesus, in the Holy Spirit, transforms us into Body and Blood of Christ and consecrates us and makes us a holy people. This is the effect of grace within and among us, if we are correctly disposed to receive it and for it to be fruitful in us.

There are, therefore three senses of the meaning of 'Amen' in this simple yet profound exchange. Ponder them next time as you walk up and stretch out your hand to receive communion.

49

Cleaning the sacred vessels

Previously, I mentioned there are a number of prayers that are said in a low voice either by a presider or a deacon. Here I am going to focus on the prayer that occurs during the cleansing of the vessels, the paten and chalice and other vessels that may have held the consecrated hosts and wine. At Mass with a deacon, it is a deacon who performs this ritual. When he is not present, it can be performed by a presbyter or acolyte.

Once communion has finished, the deacon (or other minister) standing at the altar, takes any vessels which have held the consecrated bread and he wipes any crumbs down into the chalice. He uses a purifier for this task. A purifier is a white linen cloth which is rectangular in shape used for wiping sacred vessels. If there is more than one chalice, he rinses these with a small amount of water. This water is poured into the main chalice. He then consumes all of the water, with the remains of consecrated wine and bread and then wipes out the chalice with the purifier. In some ways, it is like cleaning up after any meal.

There is a prayer which he says in a soft voice as he performs this ritual which makes the ritual so much more than cleaning up after a meal. Even though he alone speaks the words, notice that the language of 'we' still remains. He is praying this prayer on our behalf.

> What has passed our lips as food, O Lord, may we possess in purity of heart, that what has been given in time may be our healing for eternity.

The prayer refers to the Holy Communion which we have just received. The consecrated bread and wine have become the Body and Blood of Christ yet they still retain all of the elements of ordinary food. Eucharist is and remains bread and wine while also becoming at a spiritual level the real presence of Christ. The prayer hopes that we will not simply stay at the level of sense experience, of taste, texture and smell as we might with a meal that we are enjoying.

To 'possess' in this context means not owning or holding onto something but our way of apprehending or seeing it. We need to be able to take hold in some way of the awesome mystery which we have just consumed. This, faith tells is, the Body of Christ whole and entire. This is the word who became incarnate and died for us and is now risen and seated at the right hand of God the Father.

We do not possess this mystery as some intellectual proposition or idea but with the whole of our being. We encountered earlier the deep significance of heart in the symbolism found in the Scriptures and the early

Church writers. There is no part of us that is not touched by this mystery and no part of us excluded from the transformation that is possible for us, if we receive in faith.

In other places in this book, we have reflected on our dual citizenship. We are simultaneously citizens of heaven and earth. Even as we celebrate this Mass now in time, this Mass will come to an end, we simultaneously celebrate in eternity. Although now we only glimpse this eternity, its promise and fulfilment await our post mortem journey. One day we shall live in eternity which is a time without time. No past, no future – only an eternal present. No creation and no dying – only the fullness of existence and being with Being itself.

Eucharist is medicine. Jesus came to heal the sick and he came for the unrighteous not for the well and the righteous. Jesus came to find what was lost and to bring healing where there was brokenness and estrangement. Eucharist begins to work its healing of the malady of the soul called sin – sin being all those things which make us fall short of living a Christ-like life. Eucharist begins the healing process and helps to prepare us for eternal life with God.

After communion, it is easy to be distracted, or for some to even head for the door before Mass is finished. Presiders, no less than the people, can become distracted. Perhaps if we pay a little attention to this simple ritual, we might draw our minds and heart back to the awesome mystery which is now within our own bodies. We can spend a short moment in prayer hoping to possess and be possessed by the mystery.

50

Reserving the Blessed Sacrament

The Blessed Sacrament is another name for the consecrated hosts or bread. Catholics store or reserve, some of the consecrated host in a kind of large bowl with a lid that also has a stem a bit like a chalice; it is called a ciborium. The ciborium is placed in a cupboard that is called a tabernacle. Eastern Catholic Churches and Orthodox Churches also have a kind of tabernacle but these are less conspicuous than the Latin Catholic variety.

Depending on factors like the age and design of a Latin Catholic Church, the tabernacle may be in the sanctuary area behind or near the altar or in a location a little removed from the sanctuary but still accessible to the clergy and people. Sometimes, in older Churches built before the 1960s, the tabernacle is built into the high altar against the front wall of the Church. Some of these are quite elaborate in their designs and size. They were located there because for many centuries only the clergy approached the Blessed Sacrament and so the tabernacle was assessable to them when they stood at the altar.

After Vatican II, guidelines for Church architecture encouraged designers to locate the tabernacle in a place outside of the sanctuary so that the focus of the Mass would not be the tabernacle and reserved eucharist but the action of the Mass in which all were participating. The decision about the location of tabernacles is left to the guidance of the diocesan bishop.

Catholics reserve the Blessed Sacrament for two reasons. The first is to provide communion for the sick. A small supply of hosts will ensure that those who require Viaticum, food for the journey, as they approach death or who are in serious illness, will have something to receive without the presbyter having to celebrate a Mass as well. The second reason is for Eucharistic devotions such as adoration and benediction. These devotions are meant to flow from the Mass and lead the faithful to deepen their faith in the real presence of Jesus in the Mass, they are not an end in themselves but a means to that end.

There is one special case of reserving the Blessed Sacrament. On Holy Thursday Mass of the Lord's Supper, the presider needs to consecrate additional hosts, sufficient for the whole congregation to receive on Good Friday. There can be no Masses from Holy Thursday night until the Vigil Mass in the evening of Holy Saturday. To provide for the rite of communion that occurs during the Good Friday Service of the Lord's Passion (suffering), pre-sanctified hosts must be used. That gave the previous name to the Good Friday liturgy which was called the

Mass of Pre-sanctified Gifts. It was not a very accurate name because distribution of communion is only one quarter of the liturgy.

The *General Instruction on the Roman Missal* tells us that at Mass people should receive from the bread and wine consecrated at that Mass. The reserved Sacrament should only be used if there are more communicants than anticipated. In other words, the sacristan and those responsible for arranging things for Mass should make sure that there is sufficient for everyone at this Mass and a little left over for communion of the sick. No one should need every Sunday to take the ciborium out to distribute to the people, it should be left where it is in the tabernacle until the ministers run out of hosts and when any left-over hosts need to be stored.

Why is this important for understanding the Mass and praying it more deeply? For two main reasons. First, we should focus our attention on the celebration of the Mass. Mass is not a communion service. It is a live experience of a living mystery of faith in which the whole church is engaged. A communion service is a meditation on the word of God and receiving hosts from a previous participation in this living mystery. A communion service can never be equivalent to a Mass. That is, we want to focus our attention on the full, active and conscious participation of the whole Church in this liturgical moment.

Secondly, we need to remind ourselves that these other Eucharistic devotions – as beautiful and spiritual as they may be – are always secondary. If we are to truly benefit from adoration, it must lead us to a deep devotion to the celebration of the Mass. If we only focus on Christ's presence in the Eucharist – which is the focus of this adoration – we may not recognise his presence in the ordained ministers, the Scriptures proclaimed and the people assembled. When adoration renews our eucharistic faith and deeps our sensitivity to seeing Jesus in all these things, we know it is beginning to work in us.

The Eucharist is first and foremost food to fill the hunger of our souls. It should also stimulate in us a hunger for justice so that all of our sisters and brothers are able to have the essentials in life, their daily bread. The eucharist is medicine for our healing. It should serve as impetus for us to work for the healing and unity of humanity. We, the Church, are the sign and instrument of communion with God and the unity of the human race. We can adore the Blessed Sacrament reserved but we must long for consuming it. Eucharist is the food that will fill the longing in our hearts and the medicine that will heal us.

51
Moving parts – prayer after communion

After we have received communion, the main way that we continue our prayer is through singing the communion hymn or chant. The whole congregation should join in singing a Eucharistic or communion-themed hymn from the moment the procession forms until its end. After the last of the congregation has received communion, there is some quiet time during which the deacon cleans the sacred vessels and acolytes or servers remove from the altar all the items used for the Mass and place on a table which is close by.

During the cleaning up time and for a short while after, all should sit in silence. This is a time for you to offer your own silent prayer to God in thanksgiving for what you have received. Deepen your communion with the Lord whom you have received in the Eucharist.

After this brief period of silence, the presider will pray the prayer after communion. These prayers are another one of the moving parts of the Mass and a different one will be prayed on each Sunday. They will pick up themes from the feast or season and link the reception of Holy Communion with the particular aspect of the paschal mystery which we celebrate on this particular Sunday. I have included a small sample below to indicate some flavour of these prayers after communion.

First Sunday of Advent

May these mysteries, O Lord,
In which we have participated,
Profit us, we pray, for even now as we walk amongst passing things,
You teach us by them to love the things of heaven
And hold fast to what endures.
Through Christ our Lord.
Amen.

Third Sunday of Paschal/Easter Time

Look with kindness upon your people, O Lord,
And grant, we pray,
That those you were pleased to renew by eternal mysteries
May attain in their flesh
The incorruptible glory of the resurrection.
Through Christ our Lord.
Amen.

Fourth Sunday of Lent

O God, who enlighten
everyone who comes into
the world,
Illuminate our hearts we
pray,
With the splendour of your
grace,
That we may always
ponder
What is worthy and
pleasing to your majesty
And love you in all
sincerity.
Through Christ our Lord.
Amen.

Eleventh Sunday of Ordinary time

As this reception of your
Holy Communion, O Lord,
Foreshadows the union of
your faithful in you,
so may it bring about unity
in the Church.
Through Christ Our Lord.
Amen.

See how each one has a different flavour. The Advent prayer plays with the dual time and place in which we live between Christ coming among us and his return. We are people of the earth and need to be attentive to things of the earth because they can also point us toward a deeper reality to be found in God if we contemplate them with faith.

The prayer from Lent occurs on a Sunday when we read from the Gospel of John about how Christ is the light which has come into the world and we consider what it means to live in the darkness. So, we turn our minds and hearts toward what is pleasing to God as part of our Lenten journey of repentance.

The Easter prayer speaks of the Church, those who have been renewed by the sacraments, and especially the sacraments of initiation: baptism, eucharist and confirmation/chrismation. We always renew our baptismal promises at the at Easter Vigil and Easter Sunday. We ponder the mystery of our own resurrection from the dead, which brings us back to the central mystery of the Paschal season.

The prayer from Ordinary Time ponders the double effect of our receiving Holy Communion. It is both for our communion with God and the unity of the Church. Both are necessary if the Church is the sign and sacrament of intimate communion with God and the unity of the whole human race. This is a tiny sample of the prayers after communion. I hope you have captured some of the flavour and importance of this little prayer. As with all the prayers, we need to be attentive to it and perhaps ponder this prayer before and after Mass so that we deepen our appreciation of what each means. Throughout the year, each one unfolds a little more of the mystery of Holy Communion for us.

52

Sent on mission

It may seem a little odd but the name of our gathering, the Mass (*Missa*), actually means the sending. In the Latin language, in which the Mass is written (for Latin or Roman Catholics), the rite of dismissal in its simplest form is, '*Ite missa est!*' or 'Go, you are sent!' It is an order. These are not the last words of the Mass as they are closely followed by a response from the clergy and people, 'Thanks be to God'.

The rite of dismissal is not like dismissing a crowd, a company of soldiers or a school assembly. It is not simply bringing an end to the proceedings and then everyone just goes about his or her ordinary business. This is about sending people on a mission. All that we have been doing in this Mass is part of a preparation for what has to come next – living the mission.

We have been called together by God, formed by the word, transformed by the sacrament and sent on mission. Four key elements; called, formed, transformed and sent. Throughout this meditation on the Mass, we have seen elements of this pattern emerging and now we come to this conclusion. We are all sent on mission. Each one of us a missionary disciple, called to live and proclaim the Gospel in the context of our family, our work, our society and indeed for the good of the planet. Although only some are called to ministry, lay and ordained, all are called and sent on mission. Pope Benedict attempted to bring out more clearly that the rite of dismissal is actually sending the people on mission to the world. He introduced a number of new ways that the deacon, and. if there is no deacon, the presbyter can send the people on mission. The first two versions of the words of dismissal were in the original text and the last two are the ones added by Benedict XVI. During Easter, we add alleluias to the rites of dismissal.

Go forth, the Mass is ended.

Go in peace.

Go and announce the Gospel of the Lord.

Go in peace, glorifying the Lord by your life.

You can see more clearly from these last two the intention of the rite of dismissal. We are being sent to proclaim the Gospel in word and deed. Our lives are to be so transformed that our way of being gives glory to God and, through us, all will come to believe in the One whom God has sent.

Each one of us is meant to be good news (gospel) for our world. Pope Paul VI pointed out a long time ago that women and men today are unlikely to listen to our words when we proclaim the Gospel and, if they are to listen at all, it is because, first, we are witnesses to what we believe. When we live a life that is a credible sign of what we believe, then others may find us and our words credible. This is not an easy road for us. The word martyr means witness. We know from the history of our Church – including in our present day – that some are called to witness by the giving of their lives. That kind of witness will not come into the life of most Christian but we may still know the cost of discipleship in standing up for our values and beliefs and for defending the poor and vulnerable.

In the twentieth and twenty-first centuries, Christians have become one of the most persecuted religious groups on the planet. This alongside the horror of the Shoah of the Jews (sometimes called the Holocaust) in which six million Jews or more were brutally exterminated, sometimes by their Christian neighbours who may have gone to Mass on Sunday. How was such a thing possible? How does one split his/her mind so that Jews can be murdered and then come to Church to worship a Jew and take his broken body in the Eucharist? It is estimated that about eleven Christians are killed each day because they are Christian and that number continues to rise. Churches are increasingly coming under attack from vandals and being desecrated. We should keep in mind the martyrs who bear witness with their lives.

The Mass sends most of us to the ordinary work of witness and not the heroic kind in which we shed our blood. I suggest that living true to our Catholic and Christian principles can be its own kind of heroism when we live in a culture that is largely indifferent and sometimes hostile to expressions of faith. To live a life that glorifies God and proclaims the Gospel, cannot always be easy. That is perhaps why Jesus said to us, 'If anyone would come after me, let them deny themself and take up their cross daily and follow me' (Luke 9:23).

I wonder sometimes what these final words of the Mass mean, 'Thanks be to God'. Is it the Church saying thanks be to God that he sends us on mission? Is it thanking God for the whole of the paschal mystery that we have celebrated in the Mass? Is it the Church expressing its thanks that Christ remains present in his Body the Church and that, through the Holy Spirit, his works and his presence will continue? What can your 'thanks be to God mean' for you and your life as a missionary disciple?

It surprises many to learn that there is no recessional hymn indicated in the Mass of the Roman Rite. Perhaps because there is a hymn or chant to accompany the entrance procession, people just assumed there was one for the procession out of the Mass.

The Mass just ends with the last words of the people, followed by the ministers reverencing the altar with a kiss and processing out. No mention of music. We need to imagine that everyone just walks out after them and begins to do what they have just said they would do – go on mission. I have been in parishes with no recessional hymn and after the ministers pass the first row of seats, the people fall in behind and all process out together. It is a powerful symbol of the Church heading out on mission.

Now that we have come to end of our reflection on the Mass the real question becomes how will this make a difference to your living of the Gospel. Perhaps you need to start the whole journey again and retrace your steps. The poet T.S. Elliot wrote,

> 'We shall not cease from exploration,
> And the end of all our exploring,
> Will be to arrive where we started,
> And know the place for the first time.'

from *Little Gidding*.

In a similar way, the shorter, and probably original, ending of the Gospel of Mark concludes with the women being sent on a mission to tell the other disciples about the empty tomb to tell them to meet Jesus in Galilee, where it all started. But the women said nothing to no one for they were afraid... (Mark 16:8).

A final word

Now that you have come to the end of my reflections, I hope you will begin again but, this time, not with my reflections but begin to look again at your own experience of the Mass. Go back to the beginning of the Mass and retrace your journey. What do you see or hear now? Has your experienced changed? Is there something different in the way that you bring yourself to this moment and pray the Mass?

Do you have some sense of a shift in your liturgical spirituality? Is there a deeper appreciation for the Mass? Do you begin to feel connections between the Mass and your living of the Christian message? Is there a deeper awareness of your connections to the people with whom you gather? Is there a richer sense of what is means to be Church?

Are you a little more aware of your role among the priestly people celebrating the Mass? Do you have a greater understanding of what full, conscious and active participation means? Are you a little more aware that we are all saying Mass together, through, with and in Christ?

The liturgy, the Mass, can be a beautiful celebration that lifts up the mind, heart and body toward God and which allows us to sense the deep mystery and awe of communion with Christ in his body the Church. Not every parish is going to have the resources of music, readers and ministers who can create the atmosphere of mystery and deep reverence that characterise the Mass. There are still going to be experiences of Mass that are poor in the art of celebration and the quality of preaching that can make Mass a less than satisfying experience of worship. It is possible to enrich the experience of your next fifty-two Sundays by carrying within your own heart a predisposition to touch, smell, hear, see and taste the great mystery that you encounter there, even if it is only perceived dimly through the quality of celebration available in your parish?

Thank you for allowing me to accompany you over these past fifty-two Sundays. Let's accompany each other in a communion of prayer for the rest of the journey.

Words to know

This little glossary of words may be useful as you read through the book because some terms come up a number of times.

Acolyte — An adult man or woman instituted and installed by a liturgical ritual as server at Mass.

Advent — The first four weeks of the liturgical year (around November-December) which looks forward to the celebration of the birth of Christ and his coming again. The colour is purple.

Alb — A white robe that is a symbol of baptism. At Mass, it is worn by servers, acolytes and also clergy (deacons, presbyters and bishops).

Altar — The large table on which the bread and wine for Eucharist are placed and the Liturgy of Eucharist takes place.

Ambo — The large table from which the Scripture portions are read at Mass.

Bishop — The word bishop comes into English from a Koine Greek word, *episcopos*, which

	means overseer. This is the person who leads and looks over a diocese.
Cantor	Someone who leads the congregation in singing, especially the parts of the Mas and the Psalm.
Catholic Churches	There are twenty-one 'families' of Catholic Churches that are in communion with each other and the Bishop of Rome. Some of these churches are the Latin or Roman Catholic Church, the Maronite Catholic Church, Ukrainian Greek Catholic Church, Melkite Catholic Church and many others. Each Church has its own set of rites for Mass and the sacraments. To make things more confusing, in ecumenical conversations, all of the different Catholic Churches are called Roman Catholic.
Chalice	The large cup which the presider will use for the wine at Mass.
Chasuble	The outer cloak-like garment that a presbyter or bishop wears at Mass. It does not have sleeves. The colour will match a liturgical feast or season. Green for Ordinary Time, Purple for Lent and Advent, White or Gold for Easter and Christmastide.

Chrismation Eastern Catholics confirm or mark with Chrism at Baptism. Their word for confirmation is chrismation.

Christian Scriptures Some authors and books refer to the Second Testament as the Christian Scriptures. I don't and I think it is a grave error to do so. The First and Second Testaments are the Christian Scriptures. One of our first heresies was a denial that the First Testament was Christian scripture and so I strongly urge us not to reinforce an error.

Christmastide This period begins with the Solemnity of Nativity (25 December) and finishes with the Solemnity of the Baptism of Jesus (also called Theophany) around 12/13 January. There are other feasts in between such as Epiphany on 6 January. The days from December 25 to January 6 are the thirteen days of Christmas.

Ciborium A bowl-like vessel with a stem that is used for the storage of consecrated hosts.

Cincture A rope-like cord that is only used to tie a loose fitting alb around the waist.

Confirmation One of the three Catholic sacraments of initiation, Baptism and First Holy Communion being the other two.

Corporal	A large, square, white linen cloth that is placed on the altar and on which the chalice and paten are placed.
Crucifix	A cross on which the image of the body of Christ is fixed. A cross may not have an image of a body affixed and is just called a cross. Some icons have an image of a body painted onto the surface.
Dalmatic	The outer vestment of a deacon. It is a straight tunic and has sleeves.
Deacon	A deacon is an ordained minister and primarily assists the bishop in the diocese through ministry at the altar, proclaiming the word and works of charity and administration. He has a number of specific tasks within the Mass.
Diocese	A geographic area of the Catholic Church over which a bishop leads.
Easter	The fifty days from Easter Sunday to Pentecost. It is also called Paschal Time. The liturgical colour is white or gold.
Eastern Catholic Churches	The Roman Catholic Church is made up of twenty-one principal Churches. The Latin, sometimes called the Roman Church, is the largest and developed from what was the western half of the

ancient Roman Empire. It corresponds to central and western Europe today. Eastern Catholic Churches are those Churches that have their origins in the Eastern Roman Empire. Some of these Catholic Churches include the Maronite Church, the Ukrainian Greek Catholic Church, the Melkite Church, Armenian Church, Coptic Church, Chaldean Church, Syro-Malabar Church and other Catholic Churches. All of these, apart from the Maronite Church, have an Orthodox sister Church. These Churches have their own liturgical traditions, calendars, vestments and languages and their own rite for celebrating Mass and other sacraments which they call mysteries.

Eparch It is the equivalent term to a diocesan bishop in the Eastern Catholic and also Orthodox Churches.

Epiclesis A Koine Greek word meaning to call down the Holy Spirit. The presider stretches his hands over the bread and wine.

Eucharist Literally means thanksgiving. It is the name given to the consecrated bread and wine. Eucharistic prayer, Prayer of Great Thanksgiving.

Evangeliary The Book of Gospels.

First Testament	An alternative name for the Old Testament. Some people think 'old' means outdated, which it is certainly not, so I use First Testament because it was written first.
GIRM	General Instruction of the Roman Missal. A short book which offers commentary and guidance about how the Mass is to be celebrated.
Hebrew Scripture	Some authors and some books refer to the First Testament as the Hebrew Scriptures. I don't. I think it is misleading. There is a Hebrew version of the First Testament but there is also a Greek one and it is the Greek version upon which the Second Testament mostly relies.
Host	The communion bread, from the Latin *hostia* or victim.
Icon	A religious painting on which is drawn and written scenes from the life of Christ, or an image of Mary the Mother of God, the saints and others who may be venerated. Icon means image in Gree
Koine Greek	The New Testament is written in a language called Koine Greek, which means common Greek. This is a simplified form of Greek which was commonly shared among the people of the Mediterranean region at the

time of Jesus and the early Church. Most of the first Christians were Greek-speaking, even if they were Jews, and they read the Greek version of the First Testament called the Septuagint.

Latin Mass See traditional Latin Mass.

Latin or Roman Rite Most Catholics in the world are called Latin or Roman Rite Catholics. That is because they celebrate the Mass and sacraments according to the rites followed in Rome. Their Mass and all their sacramental books are written in the Latin language and translated into local languages.

Lectionary The book from which the readings for Mass are taken. It has portions of the Bible in a lectionary for week days and another one for Sundays.

Lector An adult man or woman instituted and installed through a liturgical ritual as reader at Mass.

Lent Forty days of preparation for Easter (Paschal time). The colour is purple.

Liturgy The public common worship rituals of the Church, e.g., Mass, Rite of Baptism, Rite of Christian Marriage.

Local Church An alternative name for a diocese.

Mass This is the name given to the Catholic act of worship, sometimes also called the Eucharist. Mass (*missa*) comes from the rite of dismissal in Latin, '*Ite missa est.*' or 'go, you are sent'.

Missal A missal or Mass book is a smaller version of the Roman Missal that many lay people have to refer to the texts and rituals of the Mass.

Monstrance A vessel used to display a large host that has been consecrated for the purpose of Eucharistic adoration and benediction. It will have a clear glass case (lunette) in the centre which holds the host. The lunette may be surrounded by elaborate designs. It has a stand.

New Testament See Second Testament.

Old Testament See First Testament.

Ordinary Time About thirty-five weeks of the year are Ordinary time. During this time, one Gospel is read semi-continuously throughout the year. The liturgical colour is green.

Ordo A small book that contains the calendar for the liturgical celebrations of the Eucharist and Liturgy of the Hours. In the Latin

	Catholic Churches, the Ordo is produced by each bishop's conference for their territories. It includes feasts and seasons of the general calendar and also special days, saints, etc. that are only found within this territory or celebrated there.
Paschal Candle	The large Candle which mostly sits by the baptismal font. Decorated with Easter/Paschal symbolism.
Paschal time	Jews celebrate Pesach which is Passover in English at around the time of Easter. In Greek, it is called Pascha or, in Latin, Paschal time. It is an alternative name for Easter and Easter time.
Paten	The plate on which at least the presiders host (communion bread) will be placed but other hosts could also be placed there.
Presbyter	This is a Koine Greek word and means elder. In the early Church, the presbyters acted as a council to advise the bishop. Over time, a custom grew of calling presbyters priests. A presbyter today is the priest who administers a parish and presides at Mass.
Presidents Chair	The chair on which the presbyter or bishop who is presiding at Mass will sit.

Presider	This is the presbyter or bishop who is the chief celebrant for the Mass. Most times, there will be just one presider.
Priest[1]	A presbyter is commonly called a priest. This is because one of the things a presbyter does is priestly i.e., offer the sacrifice of the Mass as the presider. A presbyter receives priestly ordination.
Priest[2]	All of the baptised are a priestly people and offer the Mass together with the presider. Deacons are ordained and are priestly, but are not ordained priests. Lay people are priestly but not ordained priests. The common priesthood.
Processional Cross	A large cross which a server carries into the Church at the head of the entrance procession and recessional.
Purifier	A rectangular white linen cloth for cleaning the chalice and paten.
Reader	A lay women or man, not instituted, who reads the Scripture portion, apart from the Gospel, at Mass.
Rite	A rite is a way of celebrating the Mass or the sacraments.
Roman Catholic	In ecumenical discussions, Roman Catholic includes Latin Rite and all other Catholic

	Churches (see Eastern Catholic above). When Catholics use Roman Catholic, it means only the Latin Rite or Roman or Western Catholics and not the Eastern Catholic Churches.
Roman Missal	The large book the presider will have on the altar which contains all of the prayers and instructions for ritual actions for Mass.
Sacramentary	The Roman Missal is sometimes called a sacramentary.
Sacristan	The room where the clergy put on their vestments and the items for Mass are stored is called the sacristy. The person who helps in putting out the things necessary for Mass is called the sacristan.
Sacristy	See sacristan.
Sanctuary Lamp	A red lamp that is near the tabernacle and symbolises the presence of God. Adopted from synagogue architecture.
Second Testament	An alternative name for the New Testament. Some people think 'new' means better, or that the 'old' is outdated, so I use Second Testament because it was written second.
Septuagint	This is the Koine Greek language version of the First Testament translated from

Hebrew. It has more books and some more sections within books than the Hebrew version, which is why Catholic and Orthodox Bibles have more books than the Protestant Bible. Protestants rely on the Hebrew version. The first Christian communities used the Septuagint and almost always quote from that version and not the Hebrew language version of the Bible.

Server — A male or female child or adult who assists the acolyte, deacon or presider at Mass.

Stole — A band of cloth signifying ordained office. A deacon wears his over the left shoulder and joins at the waist. A presbyter or bishop wears it around his neck and hanging down the front.

Tabernacle — The cupboard in which the consecrated hosts are stored after Mass. It may be in the sanctuary or some other place.

Traditional Latin Mass — The Mass which is celebrated in every Latin or Roman Rite Catholic parish, every Sunday, is the traditional Latin Mass. It is written in Latin and translated into various languages. It comes to us from the tradition of the Catholic Church. This is the ordinary form of the traditional

Latin Mass. The extraordinary for of this Mass is the one celebrated immediately prior to the Second Vatican Council. It can be used under specific circumstances.

Tridentine — *Tridentine* refers to the Council of Trent (1545-65) from the Latin name of the City of Trent, *Tridentium*.

Tridentine Mass — Sometimes people refer to the Mass that was commonly celebrated by most Roman or Latin Catholics before the reforms of Vatican II as the Tridentine Mass. That is not quite correct. Trent did not develop a single Mass but simply ordered that the many forms of Mass be brought into greater harmony and needless repetitions or superstitious elements be removed. Some religious orders, like the Dominicans, had their own rite of Mass, so there were multiple versions of Masses after the Council of Trent.

The Council of Trent did not mandate Latin for the language of Mass. The Council taught that Mass can be celebrated in any language but that those who claim that ' if Mass is celebrated in Latin, it is not valid', they are incorrect.

Further reading

Many of these resources would be available from an online bookseller if you do not have a bookshop or library near you. Most of the papal documents are available free online.

Benedict XVI *Sacramentum Caritatis: The Sacrament of Love*. 2007 St Pauls Publications: Strathfield.

Cantalamessa, R. *The Eucharist Our Sanctification*. 1993 Liturgical Pres: Collegeville, Minn.

Chupungco, A. *What, Then, Is the Liturgy? Musings and Memoir*. 2010 Liturgical Pres: Collegeville, Minn.

Collins, G. *Meeting Christ in His Mysteries: A Benedictine Vision of the Spiritual Life*. 2010 Liturgical Pres: Collegeville, Minn.

Congar, Y. *At the Heart of Christian Worship: Liturgical Essays of Yves Congar*. Trans by Paul Philibert. 2010 Liturgical Pres: Collegeville, Minn.

Congregation for Divine Worship and Sacraments *General Instruction on the Roman Missal: Final Text with Application for Australia*. 2012 St Pauls Publications: Strathfield

Ganozy, A. *An Introduction to Catholic Sacramental Theology*. 1984 Mosaic press: Preston, Victoria.

Further reading

Hahn, S. *The Lamb's Supper: The Mass as Heaven on Earth.* 1999 Darton, Longman & Todd: London.

John Paul II *Ecclesia de Eucharistia: On the Eucharist and its Relationship to the Church.* 2003 St Pauls Publications: Strathfield.

———— *Apostolic Letter on the Sacred Liturgy.* 1989. St Pauls Publications: Strathfield.

———— *Mane Nobiscum Domine: For the Year of the Eucharist.* 2004. St Pauls Publications: Strathfield.

———— *Novo Millennio Ineunte: At the Beginning of the new Millennium.* 2001 St Pauls Publications: Strathfield.

McCann, C. *101 Liturgical Suggestions Practical Ideas for Those who Prepare the Liturgy.* 2014 Veritas: Dublin

McEvoy, J., Hogan, M. (eds) *The Mystery of Faith: Reflections on the Encyclical Ecclesia de Eucharistia.* 2005 Columba press: Dublin.

Pecklers, K. *The Genius of the Roman Rite: The Reception and Implementation of the New Missal.* 2009 Burns and Oats: London.

Rosse, G. *The Spirituality of Communion: A New Approach to the Johannine Writings.* 1998. New City Writings: New York.

Sri, E. *A Biblical Walk Through the Mass: Understanding What we Say and Do in the Liturgy.* 2010 Ascension Press: West Chester, PA.

Turner, P. *Ars Celebrandi: Celebrating and Concelebrating Mass*. 2021 The Liturgical press: Collegeville, Minn.

———— *At the Supper of the Lamb A Pastoral and Theological Commentary on the Mass*. 2011 Liturgy Training Publications.

www.ingramcontent.com/pod-product-compliance
Lightning Source LLC
Chambersburg PA
CBHW012003090526
44590CB00026B/3859